Shoeless Soccer Fixing the System and Winning the World Cup

Carlo Celli, Nathan Richardson

D1554975

1

Table of Contents

Preface

15. No Quality

16. No Worries

Preface

In 2010, over three million American children played organized soccer, the number-one participation sport in America, surpassing football, baseball, and even basketball. Such numbers led to prognostications of imminent greatness. The World Cup semifinals were just a generation away. The finals? Maybe two. The American Messi was on the horizon, and the sky was the limit.

Or so they said.

Today, we've crashed back to earth. Despite the inspiration of a handful of young Americans abroad, there is still no American Messi, and the US men's national team not only will not play in the semifinals of the 2018 World Cup, they won't even be at the tournament. Most damning of all is the recent revelation that by 2016, despite the continued overall growth of the US population, the number of kids playing soccer did not just stagnate but declined by nearly twenty-five percent![1]

What went wrong?

Or, more importantly, what *is* wrong?

For nearly two decades now, we have observed youth soccer in America at close quarters. We've been parents to kids who have played everything from parks and recreation and local competitive soccer to regional select and high school. Over those same years we've coached dozens of teams at a variety of levels. We've seen scores of the kids advance through the system, including to all levels of college soccer. Completing the circle, some of our former players are now coaches themselves.

Over this same period, both of us have had the opportunity for frequent travel around the world. On several occasions, we have resettled our families for summers and entire school years in soccer-mad nations. Specifically, we have seen our own kids train and play in the Italian and Spanish youth systems. Whenever we visit a country, we make it a point to check out youth practices, games, and afternoon playground shoot-arounds. When we return home, we compare notes and wonder why we can't do that in the States.

What we've observed and concluded thus far is shared in the following pages. While we have decades of playing, coaching, and club administrative experience between us, not to mention a host of USSF and NSCAA coaching licenses, we don't claim the expertise of the elite perched at the top of the US Soccer pyramid. Our livelihoods are not dependent on the US soccer club system.

This means we can tell you something they cannot: the truth.

What we do claim is the very perspective from the bottom, built on watching and coaching for thousands of hours at America's grassroots level and then drawing comparisons to what we see overseas.

We wrote this because what we see from that bottom-up, comparative view is not pretty. The behemoth that is US Youth Soccer is a beast without teeth or, if you will, an emperor without clothes. Our kids are arguably the best-dressed youth players in the world. They train on the "best" fields, are directed by the "best" coaches, and are driven to and from practices in the "best" soccer-mom SUVs. Yet beneath all those expensive uniforms and trappings, there's simply not much skill. In the American soccer system, "best" is not for the best, and more has become less. With that in mind, over the following pages, we'll undress the corrupted and expensive American version of what, around the world, is called the beautiful game. We'll strip it down to its essence, rip off the shin guards, unlace the shoes, tear up the fields, toss out the coaches, and shut down the club system.

"The Shoeless Ones" was the first team of Pele, the greatest footballer of all time. Ironically, Pele and his teammates became good and even great players because of, rather than despite their lack of shoes and equipment. In their honor, we'll take the world's game of football back to its roots, to the streets, vacant lots, and patios where kids play and creativity flourishes. In the process, we'll save ourselves a lot of time and money. That's a good thing because we'll need that cash years from now when at last (thank goodness) we'll happily fork some of it out for those front row seats to the US men's national teams' first World Cup final. Because, from what we've seen in our world travels and in our travails on the fields of America's youth soccer programs, once we start playing what we'll be calling *shoeless soccer* in honor of its stripped-down approach, the sky's the limit.

So sit down, relax, kick off your shoes (not to mention that expensive travel uniform), and prepare to see soccer from the bottom up. To see the mess we've made and, more importantly, the radically simple solutions for getting us, at last, to the top. Get ready to go shoeless.

1. No Grass

Are We Growing Kids or Growing Grass?

One of my first seasons as a soccer coach, on a glorious and surprisingly warm mid-spring evening at the end of another long, cold Midwestern winter, we took our Boys' under-nine (U9) team up the highway for a midweek travel game with a local rival. The boys were starting to put together some decent soccer. We were excited to play, but when we arrived at the fields, no one was there. No worries, we thought, we'll get in some extra touches before the other guys arrive. So we did, that is, until the cops showed up.

"Fields are closed. You all need to pack up and get off the grass… Everyone, now."

We looked on, a bit stunned: the players, their families, and the grandparents, their folding chairs just set down, settled in to enjoy a gorgeous spring afternoon of youth soccer. Being fairly new to the sport, none of us quite knew what was going on. Instead of moving, we stood there staring at the officer figuring there must be some mistake. The officer, hands on hips, approached.

"The fields are closed, you've gotta leave."

"What's the matter?" we asked.

"The fields are wet. They've been closed to protect the grass. You've gotta get off. Now."

We stared in disbelief. Wet? We'd been there for ten minutes. Living in the Midwest, we were very familiar with wet soccer fields. We lived on them. These were definitely not wet. So probably pushing things further than necessary—not yet understanding how *pratophilia* (love of fields) had become *pratomania* (obsession with fields) in the soccer world I had recently joined—I immediately fell to my butt, deciding to become object lesson number one for the enforcing officer.

"But these fields are dry as a bone, officer. Look, I'm seated on my keister, right here. Totally dry." I stood up and showed him my utterly dry backside.

"Sorry," the officer replied, "Due to heavy rains all fields are closed. Time to leave."

By that point, we were beginning to understand. We packed up and left. The parents were a bit peeved. The kids were crushed. And I was much wiser. My final words to the officer, as we walked, away have stayed with me as, unfortunately, something I've had to repeat time and again over the years.

"Are we growing kids or growing grass?"

Sadly, the honest answer to the question continues to be, all too often, the latter, and the obsession is only growing. In our neck of the woods our local parks and rec department used to let our community soccer club use city fields free of charge. Moreover they let us determine whether the fields were playable. Typically if there wasn't a typhoon, we played—and to be clear, the fields survived. Today the same club pays the city ever-higher fees for increasingly well-manicured lawns that half the time we can no longer use. The creep began nearly a decade ago when the parks and rec sports specialist—an indoor basketball enthusiast with really no soccer experience to speak of—unilaterally decided to make the calls on soccer fields. Almost overnight we began to experience frequent cancellations. Within a couple of years, the sports specialist, again without warning or explanation, turned field decisions over to the city lawn specialist, a well-meaning but utterly soccer-ignorant government employee whose sole job was to manage the town's fields. He was the lawn guy. To him, any divot, any worn-down patch, any muddy goal mouth, understandably, just meant more work.

Predictably the fields began to be closed more often than they were open.

And so, time and again I found myself standing in parks and rec meetings or out on "unplayable" fields fruitlessly negotiating with basketball gurus and grass growers. Every discussion ended with the same question, "Are we growing kids or growing grass?"

It's Complicated, or Is It?

Of course we're growing kids, you may argue. Our interest is with kids playing soccer, learning and developing and growing their love for the game. But, you insist, we need grass to play the game. The better the lawn the better the soccer. After all, check out the fields at the best soccer venues around the world. You'll see some serious lawn care. If we want great soccer, we're obliged to take care of the means that will lead to that end. Hence, *pratomania*.

Unfortunately, there's one big problem with that answer.

And, ironically, that problem begins with the grass itself.

So let's step back and ask ourselves, what's with our grassy obsession in the first place?

First, let's acknowledge that professional soccer games at the highest level are played on grass—well, unless you're a female athlete. (In which case you make due with artificial turf. Why? Because, well, apparently you don't quite measure up, despite the arguments of all those USA World Cup trophies to the contrary.)

Second, let's acknowledge, furthermore, that the game originated on grass, invented in England on the finely manicured lawns of Eaton and other rival nineteenth-century boys' schools.

11

Lovely arguments. Except, of course, they don't actually work. At least, if you're interested in playing good soccer. Think for a moment, while we concede the point.

Two (False) Concessions

Concession one: Yes, world-class soccer is played on grass. Concession two: Yes, soccer was invented on grass.

In both cases, however, let us first consider the grass in professional stadiums across the globe. What does a World Cup stadium pitch look like? How about Barcelona FC's Camp Nou? Have you ever played on just about any professional pitch or even on a reasonably manicured NCAA Division-I field? Think about it. How does that lawn compare to our kids' typical practice fields?

While we keep that in mind, let's turn to the fields where the game was first invented. Anyone ever slog across the thick, chewed-up lawns of nineteenth-century boys' schools dotting the heaths and moors of the British Isles? What are those lawns like?

Now a bit of history. The rules of soccer, or Association Football as the rule-makers originally called it, were first recorded for posterity at the Freemasons' Tavern in central London in November 1863. The event was a meeting of representatives of eleven old boys' clubs in the London area. The eleven were determined once and for all to make sense of the competing footballing styles evolving across the British Isles. The styles ranged widely and wildly but could, in general, split the schools into two groups: those who favored kicking and those who favored carrying the ball. The groups favoring the kicking game ended up agreeing that day at the tavern on the rules that would come to be known as Association Football. Those who walked away from the meeting disgruntled were the proponents of carry, toss, and tackle (we're talking NFL-style tackling). This latter group would soon codify their own rules charting the course of the sport known today as Rugby. (NFL-style football is yet another story).

With that in mind, can we pause for a moment and imagine what those Eaton versus Rugby football matches must have looked like? Imagine the beatings those pitches must have taken and the battle scars they must have borne day after day under the rainy English skies. How many muddy patches, puddles, even ponds, would have dotted that field the last time Eaton and Rugby stood face-to-face before realizing something had to be done about all the wild innovations from school to school and the resulting disagreements? How would a ball have travelled under such conditions? What would the game they were playing have looked like? What skills would it have encouraged?

Back home to our own thought experiments, have any of us ever attempted to play soccer on a Rugby pitch? Of course it can be done. So perhaps a better question would be whether any of us has ever tried to play Barcelona-style *tiki-taka* soccer—the kind that makes FIFA World Players of the Year, take you to Champions League finals, and crowns World Cup victors—on a Rugby pitch? Chew on that.

And while we chew on that, let's think about the place that made *tiki-taka* famous, Barça's famous Camp Nou. This lawn that produced the most recent innovation in soccer, an innovation that has led to the rethinking of how we teach and play the game. It's the style of soccer that has inspired successive revisions of US Soccer's own curriculum to emphasize technical skills above all else. The way Barça played under coach Pep Guardiola from 2008 to 2012 and the way Spain—with many of those same Barça players—played and won two consecutive Euros and a World Cup in between (an unprecedented run of success) was through almost total ball possession. The best defense, they determined, was simply to deny the other team the ball.

Soccer historians recount that the legendary Uruguayan club, Peñarol, would pick up the game ball at the beginning of their matches, walk over to players on the opposing squad, and challenge them with the taunt, "Did you bring your own ball?"

The opposition, taken aback, would nonetheless answer that of course they had. The Peñarol players would wryly respond, "Good, because this one is ours."

The clear message? "You're not gonna touch this ball. We're so good that you're never going to get it from us."

As anyone who has ever played soccer well knows, that kind of possession requires special technical skills. But those kinds of skills work only on a certain kind of pitch.

And how must that pitch be?

Pep Guardiola, the famed Barça coach, is well known for his meticulous instructions for pitch care: blades of grass no longer than 1.5 cm (recall, one inch is 2.54 cm). If Pep has his suspicions, he'll step out on the pitch in the middle of a game with a ruler. He knows the kind of lawn good football demands. His teams need to play the best football possible. So 1.5 cm it is.

Think about how long—or short—1.5 cm is. Short enough to be practically carpet. Now to be fair, not everyone is as obsessed with perfect pitches as Pep. The equally famous manager José Mourinho, one of Guardiola's more bitter rivals, has argued that there are other ways to play soccer and that these, in turn, demand a different length of grass. Mourinho prefers the grass a bit longer: a healthy 3 cm![1]

Now while that might be a dream for most of us, for Pep, that's absolutely unacceptable. And did we mention that for good measure, Pep prefers that every pitch be watered down minutes prior to every game as well as at half-time? The pitch must not just look like a carpet, but also be wet. The ball zips across the pitch, fast and hard to handle, except by the world's best, of course.

So is this one particularly eccentric coach? Well, consider that what worked for Barça, despite Mourinho's protests to the contrary, quickly spread across the globe. When Brazil was preparing to host the 2014 World Cup, they appointed as their ambassador the original Ronaldo (not Cristiano). He reports, "The first thing I did when they named me ambassador was ask for all the stadiums to have the grass like in Europe, short and fine."[2]

And where did Ronaldo play the majority of his European soccer? Barcelona, Inter Milan, and then Barça's biggest rival, Real Madrid. He knew the Camp Nou and other pitches of similar specifications intimately. So we can be confident that when Ronaldo demanded European grass he was not asking for the muddy lawns of Eaton and Blackheath. He wanted fields that are hard, fast, and maybe even a little bit wet.

So what's the takeaway from these two visits to two different lawns—those of Eaton and the Camp Nou?

The football lawns that make us think we must take care of our American soccer lawns look nothing like the lawns we're currently fussing over! In the case of the lawns on which soccer was invented, I'd venture to guess none of us are interested in playing even a pick-up game on that muddy morass. Think of the twisted ankles. Think of the poor technique and tactics lousy fields reward. Those remedial techniques and tactics do not transfer onto smooth, slick pitches. No wonder US soccer is failing!

What about the lawns we aspire to play on: the Camp Nou, Real Madrid's Santiago Bernabeu, or even that of the nearest NCAA Division-I school? They look nothing at all like the fields where our kids are learning to play. The closer to the highest technical level of soccer—in the last generation that of Barça's Messi, Xavi, Iniesta, and company—the closer the grass gets to carpet. Or dirt, or perhaps a parking lot, a patio, or a street. The surface is terribly short, terribly slick, and terribly fast. Unforgiving to all but the most skilled player.

Unsurprisingly, those are the kinds of pitches—or patios, plazas, and vacant lots—where the world's best players and best teams formed from soccer's very beginning.

In the beginning? But didn't we say the game originated with Eaton and friends? Well, that's certainly where the rules were laid down. But to get past our grassy obsessions, we need to lay aside our colonial complex with British soccer. Let's recognize that post-1863 Association Football in England was played on thick, wet, and muddy pitches. They kept playing the soccer under the eleven rules drawn up in November 1863. The rest of the world moved on. The soccer we aspire to, the world's game, the celebrated *jogo bonito* evolved far from the cliffs of Dover.

Consider for a moment who we mean when speaking of football's early greats—both players and teams. Uruguay of the 1924 and 1928 Olympics and the first ever World Cup in 1930. The Italian squads that won World Cups in 1934 and 1938 with a core of five ex-patriot *oriundi* from Uruguay's across-the-river neighbor, Argentina. At the club level we celebrate the Uruguayan outfit Peñarol, Argentina's 1940s River Plate "machine," or Brazil's Flamengo—an early iconoclast with its signings of players of African descent. And stars? How about the Austrian Matthias Sindelar, the Brazilian Leonidas da Silva, the Hungarian Francesc Puskas, the Brazilian Garincha, or the Argentine Alfredo Di Stefano. These are the names that roll off the tongues of soccer historians when considering the original greats.

What do all these early stars have in common? Certainly not thick, lush lawns.

Ah, but wait, you say, I've been to Austria. Or at least I've seen *The Sound of Music* a half-dozen times—and there's plenty of grass there. Sure. For the Von Trapp family living in the Salzburg countryside. But not for the son of a poor blacksmith. Young Sindelar was forced to play his soccer, to hone his game—long before arriving on the relatively pristine pitches of professional clubs—on the streets of Vienna's "grim industrial suburb of *Favoriten*."[3] Again, the great soccer and the great players from the beginning of the beautiful game's days were developed on… dirt, concrete, and cobble stones.

The term "pitch" is from cricket, baseball's English ancestor, which has wickets (sticks of wood) that replicate tree stumps on a field—the ancestor of home base on a baseball diamond. The origins of the English football pitch are bucolic and rural. The game that spread around the world was urban, played on hard surfaces by kids who did not have lawns or stumps, pitches or wickets.

So before we proceed, here's some food for thought. What would a soccer player who learned to play on a hard-packed dirt surface or a ceramic tiled courtyard, look like?

How would he or she be different from the kids we're developing on the lush parks-and-recky lawns across the good ol' US of A?

Soccer Spreads

We often fetishize the wrong part of England's role in soccer. Sure, they invented the game. But that really wasn't so hard to do. What they invented wasn't so unique. Kicking a ball, or an apple or a pig's head, with your feet and then finding someone to kick the ball in the opposite direction and then deciding to turn the kick-about into a competition isn't rocket science. Yes, the English codified some rules. But there's no patent on kicking things. The only reason Eve took so long to take a bite of the apple is probably that Adam was always kicking them to a pulp before she could sink her teeth into one. So, hurrah for England but, really, not that big a deal.

England's truly great contribution to soccer is the spread of the game. The codification and then popularization of Association Football in England happened to coincide conveniently with the era of Great Britain's furthest imperial reach. In the late nineteenth and early twentieth century, the British Empire spanned the globe, from the West to the East Indies passing through huge swathes of Africa and the Indian subcontinent. Where there was no formal empire, the British navy and their massive fleet of merchant vessels called at just about every port on the planet. Once ashore, the sailors played Association Football or soccer. In these ports, the story goes, local dockworkers and especially local street kids learned the game by watching and then joining in with their British visitors.

And so more food for thought: what would that first soccer game in the port of Buenos Aires, for example, have looked like? Where and how would the sailors have played?

While it is true that Buenos Aires is in the heart of the South American Pampas where grass grows naturally, anyone who has spent much time in a port can tell you there's not much lush grass growing there. But there is no shortage of pavement or cobble stones. Or perhaps simply hard-packed dirt. Of course, there would be ship decks— also unlikely to be covered in grass. All surfaces rather hard and very slick. (What would our city grass managers do with such pitches?)

Despite such theoretically inhospitable surfaces, the sailors and their protégés played, over and over again, eventually forming clubs, and then developing a game that would quickly transform the sport. Again, what would that game have looked like being played on such unforgiving surfaces? How would the ball travel? How would players attack and defend? How would they move across the pitch? What kinds of techniques would such surfaces favor? And what kind of soccer would most definitely not work out there?

Unsurprisingly, when England finally deigned to join the rest of the world on the soccer pitch in 1950, they were roundly and soundly defeated, if not humiliated.[4] Something changed while the Brits had continued hoofing long balls up their muddy, thick-grassed pitches to thick-limbed beasts fighting through mud and scrum to catch the bloody object before remaining hopelessly stuck in the quagmire at the other end.

The Argentines, the Uruguayans, the Brazilians, the Italians, the Spaniards, and the Hungarians had found a new partner—the ball—on a new dance floor, almost as slick as the burnished tango parquets in the local dive bars of the Argentine Boca. They had learned to spin and feint and dip with that ball. To caress, flick, and spin it on the tips of toes and knees and nose. They made those slick, hard-packed surfaces of dirt and brick into a brand new friend. Then when satisfied, they deftly flicked the ball to a companion who started his own dance.

No wonder the game they brought back to England half a century later, the game with which they'd been dazzling fans in World Cups since 1930, had little to do with the beastly smash-mouth breeding ground for hardened British soldiers envisioned by the headmasters nearly a century earlier. The game had become much slicker, much faster, much more brilliant, and yet much more controlled. England was at a loss, and when they tried to compete with the rest of the world after WWII, as we saw above, they lost. Badly.

With the exception of one World Cup victory, the games "originators" have underperformed ever since. But that's because the game that beat them wasn't really their game, eleven simple rules notwithstanding. The football that beat them was the game of their political and economic colonies, ripped away from the grass, reinvented for a harder, slicker, faster surface.

Since that first English re-encounter with "their" game, they and those who imitate them continue to be humiliated by the heirs of the new football developed in their old overseas haunts. The Brazilian *jogo bonito* of Garincha, Pele, and company in the 1950s and 1960s, the Dutch Total Football of the 1970s, and most recently the *tiki-taka* of Barcelona and Spain, have conquered the silverware and hearts of the world. These are the heirs of hard, unforgiving surfaces.

But surely, you might ask, the time of hard-packed dirt pitches and tiled patios has passed?

Well, kind of. Let's look at the case of Spain. Anyone taking a tour of Spanish soccer facilities today will acknowledge that the dirt of yesteryear has been replaced by field after field of artificial turf. In the last decade or so Spanish clubs, but mainly the Spanish footballing federation, invested in upgrading facilities at youth soccer venues across the country. Let us note first that their investment was not in grass seed and sprinkler systems, but in artificial turf. The stuff that in length and slickness most closely approximates the pitches at the Camp Nou, the Santiago Bernabeu, and the Sánchez Pijuán. No one in Spain is interested in replicating the pitches at Eaton, to say nothing of the thick grassy lawns of suburban American parks and rec playgrounds. Spain went straight from dirt to artificial turf.

But actually that's only half true. The dirt came in the afternoons at local clubs when little Sergio, Xavi, or Andrés of the famed Barça teams of the early 2000s were just first graders. Every day, before passing through the club gate, every weekend after the midday meal or before going in for the evening, where was that generation cutting their *tiki-taka* teeth? On the unforgiving cement of school playgrounds and neighborhood soccer courts, on the slick cobblestones of the street out back, and on the tile surfaces of the patio beneath their apartment blocks. If dirt is hard and fast, imagine a cement playground well burnished by generations of shuffling and feinting, of skipping feet, of toes dancing with a ball as if on a tether. That's where Spain's golden generation learned to play. The *tiki-taka* that conquered the world was a game invented on rock. No wonder Pep Guardiola insisted on keeping the Camp Nou grass cut to no more than 1.5 cm. Any longer, and his players wouldn't have known what to do. Rugby scrum, lads?

By the way, did we mention the Spanish tradition of inflating the ball to the point of bursting? A rock-hard ball on a nearly rock-hard surface. Again, we insist, how would that affect your game?

But What's in It for Me?

Think about the questions we've asked above and consider what a game looks like under such conditions. Consider the work of a coach. Or the lack thereof.

Does a coach need to teach ball control on a hard-packed surface? On such a pitch, ball control is a simple matter of survival. Your ability to control the ball is a question of life and death, of playing or not playing. A four-year-old out on the asphalt either figures out in the first five minutes how to control that ball or goes home and sticks to crayons and coloring books. Ball control, expert dribbling, and deft touch with every legal surface of the body—not for the sake of showing off but for the sake of simply playing the game—becomes not merely one thing among many in the early days of learning, but the *only* thing.

Now contrast that with the skills rewarded, and then unfortunately encouraged, on a lush green lawn. In the grass of too many North American soccer pitches, the ball conveniently sits. We drop it and there it rests. Immobile.

For a three-year-old to move that large round thing from one tuft to the next requires great effort, hard-plowing through a thick forest of fetishized, carefully cultivated weeds. (What's a weed anyway? A plant you don't want. Point made.) All that being the case, a kid quickly realizes the advantage to just kicking that thing as hard as you can, and preferably in the air. Then chase. Three cheers for the big kid with the big boot. Maybe a trophy too. After all, he's the only one who can seem to break up the scrum.

Come to think of it, how does that scrum even happen? If that ball were actually able to roll—say on hard-packed dirt, pavement, or a parquet surface—there probably wouldn't be much of a scrum. No need for coaches to spend five years yelling (mostly in vain) at the kids to spread out, to stay in their positions, or whatever. The ball would take care of that business in about five minutes, squirting quickly, wildly around the field. Little Johnny doesn't need to be told to get wide. He's figured out through a little observation (the kind of higher-level thinking ideally suited to a three-year old) that that's where the ball's going to be in a second or two. As soon as the next kid gets a touch, the ball rolls, and fast. So begins the wide-open passing game. And you, the coach, didn't have to say anything.

Now let's consider, in contrast, what kind of passes work on a hard-packed pitch. Big long super smashes from the oversized kid who will probably end up being average-sized once everyone catches up? (Which by then will be too late for him to ever develop any real soccer skills.) Of course not. Imagine the bounce on that hard dirt once that big-kicked ball finally lands. Imagine the chase as the ball travels another ten, twenty, or fifty yards across the adjoining fields. After five minutes the kids get the picture.

Play on a hard surface instead invites happier musings. Imagine, instead of the big kick over thick muddy lawns, the simplicity and beauty of a quick short pass on the ground that even a toddler can make look pretty. Ah, look how the ball skids gently across the surfaces to the awaiting foot of a teammate who discovered within the first five minutes of practice how to control the ball. In another five minutes that same toddler might even recognize the advantage of waiting five yards to the side for the ball that will surely squirt out on that slick, fast-moving surface. Ball control, short passes, spacing. Lo and behold we have football, *o jogo bonito*, the world's game!

But wait, there's more! Which begins, of course, with more food for thought. Ever fallen hard on a hard-packed dirt surface? Well, if you've fallen on a hard-packed dirt surface then, well, you've fallen hard, which doesn't feel good. After a single fall, you are unlikely to do it again. You figure out how to avoid falling and you adjust your game. Any of us who grew up playing any sort of games on elementary school blacktop understand. We came home once or twice with skinned knees. But not every day. There's a reason basketball, for all the advances since the days of James Naismith evolved away from the physicality of the early cagers. Falling on a hard basketball court hurts. Same with a hard-packed soccer pitch.

If you've ever coached kids between the ages of three and nine or so, you know that as with the mob-ball stuff, you spend a ridiculous amount of time trying to keep them on their feet and off their butts. It's all too tempting to fall all over that ball and make the muck of mobbed-up bodies all that much muckier when the surface is so cushiony soft. If falling doesn't hurt so much, well then, we can all play that much more recklessly. Especially that big kid with the big boot.

So the children of the grass learn to mob and learn to fall. They learn to beat on each other. The headmasters of Eaton et al, with their interests in muscular Christianity fostered through competitive, ultraphysical athletics, would be proud. What fine little soldiers we're growing for the

British Empire. Except this ain't England and we're not raising soldiers, however noble that profession might be.

No, our intent is to teach our kids to play soccer. Some of us may secretly hope our kid turns out to be the next Pele. Others may simply feel that if we're going to sign our kids up for anything—violin lessons, let's say—we'd hope that there would be some quality instruction. Then, if our children decide someday to continue, at least they'll have a solid foundation (the old, if you're going to do something, you might as well do it right shtick). Some of us may just want to give our kids something to keep them busy and a bit winded once or twice a week in the afternoons.

Whatever the case, we probably would prefer that our kids learn to play the beautiful game, the one that has taken the world by storm over the past hundred years or so, rather than the ugly, muddy thing that became in one iteration what we now call Rugby. (Again, nothing against Rugby; but if that's what you're into, play Rugby. You wouldn't want your little Rugby player to spend the entire practice learning to juggle a soccer ball now, would you?)

Lose the Lawns, Win the Game

And so, why our obsession with grass? Why are we canceling so many games and practices to preserve a surface that, as we've seen, is teaching all the wrong things? Why are we paying our parks and rec programs to use their spongy, skill-killing pitches? Why are these same parks and rec departments, often at our behest, incurring significant debt to purchase and then develop more and more acres of the grassy morass where soccer development comes to die?

Let's save the taxpayers some money.

Let's save the kids.

And let's save US Soccer while we're at it.

So, what to do? In most cases, the answer may be just out your front door. Is this country not already paved coast-to-coast with blacktop surfaces? Haven't you noticed that stuff surrounding nearly every schoolyard in the nation, increasingly sitting fallow as after-school kids stay indoors huddled around their electronic devices? What about the empty parking lots behind every place of worship or surrounding the increasingly abandoned local mall. What about their empty store spaces themselves, these days not even filled during the Christmas shopping season? These are all great places for training year-round.

How hard would it be to get the local elementary to allow you to schedule regular practices on their blacktop? Based on my every-afternoon survey of the local elementary down the street, playing on blacktop seems to be a lost art. Yet the legal mechanisms must surely be in place to put them to use. After all, that is where many of us middle-aged folks learned the fine arts of basketball and even football and softball/baseball, and not just in after-school pickups with our friends but as part of organized teams. Yes, we used to hold organized practices on blacktop. Remember when?

Now, would a switch to blacktop soccer require other changes? Sure, but that's why there are a few more chapters to this book.

For now, if we continue on the present course (like our mentors the Brits did for the past hundred plus years), then to expect different results is, as they say, the definition of insanity. It's certainly not working.

So why dump even more money into US youth soccer for even fancier grass fields?

What about copying the Spanish model with artificial turf for everyone? Artificial turf would be a wonderful solution. But while feasible in a handful of cities and clubs with the means, artificial turf is not an option for the vast majority of our young players, and it won't be where most of our three-year-olds start. Right now we need to develop the rising tide (every last US youth player) that will lift the boats to take us to the World Cup final. Right now we need to get off the grass.

US Soccer has dedicated tremendous resources over the last couple of decades to raising its game. So far, those resources have gone to Olympic Development Programs, then to the US Soccer Development Academy, the MLS academy teams, and a handful of similarly officially approved academies. We're confident those are wonderful places with highly trained coaches attempting to implement the very latest and greatest training techniques and game tactics from the best clubs the world over. But those handful of coaches and technical directors at the national level can't make a silk purse out of a sow's ear. They need a rising tide of silk.

The future stars need a nation of their peers to compete against. They will not reach the top on their own. They need all of us. We need all of us. That future star might be your kid. Or your kid might be the one to challenge and to raise his game. Or the kid challenged by the kid, challenged by your kid. Whoever it is, they—we—need each other to develop a world-class game.

US Soccer needs radical change not so much at the top as at the grassroots, where millions and millions of kids play. Ironically, grassroots transformation will best begin by ripping up the grass at the roots. When the conditions change, the game will change.

So let the lawns grow. Or go to seed. Or do whatever the local grounds crew wants them to do. We're in a different business. We're growing soccer players. We're growing footballers. We're growing kids.

2. No Shoes

How's That Toe Feeling Now?

On a frigid winter day, kids from a local team and their coach gathered in a basketball gym to play indoors. No pretenses about developing great talent or professional footballers. Just some kids, eight- to ten-year-olds whose parents wanted them to do something besides play video games and watch television.

The kids, arriving after school, were not that excited about another "practice," another helicopter-parent organized activity, another round of lectures and drills not much different from what they had experienced all day in school.

The game began in the American style with errant passes and long balls. Then play halted. One of the kid's shoes fell apart, a hand-me-down from his older brother. The sole flipped up into the air after the kid kicked the ball. His teammates laughed.

The boy's father grumbled that he would have to get the kid another pair of shoes. The other parents nodded when he said, "When I was a boy, I only had one pair of shoes and I turned out fine." Every kid nowadays needed cleats, indoor shoes, turf shoes, running shoes, basketball shoes, dress shoes, slippers, and winter boots.

The boy's broken shoe could be repaired, but not immediately. Nobody had superglue handy. Rather than exclude the now shoeless boy from play, someone suggested playing barefooted.

For the first fifteen minutes, the parents on the sidelines writhed with preoccupation about broken toes and black toenails. The kids were in the same frame of mind. Kicking the ball without shoes or socks hurt. They were also not prepared for what can happen when two bare feet hit each other. They grimaced and trotted about gingerly on the cold parquet floor, kicking the ball uncertainly, unaccustomed to the new sensations on their naked toes and heels.

Then something fortuitous happened. Initial trepidation waned. The sound and tempo of the game changed. The kids began to laugh and scamper about, aware of the feeling of freedom from contact with the ground. The coach stopped barking commands and encouragement, and just watched. There were fewer fouls. Every kid on the court hesitated before poking a foot out at an opponent. Putting a bare toe out in front of a moving ball and trampling feet was asking for trouble.

Players began to lift their chins and look about the court to judge their next move, wary of stubbing a toe, bruising a shin, or wasting the sting that came with barefooted contact with the ball on an errant trap, pass, or shot. Players began to move away from each other to get into open spaces, rather than bunching up.

One kid, trained from birth to wear socks and shoes, steadfastly refused to join play. When he saw the others enjoying themselves, he reluctantly removed his footwear and trotted onto the court. As luck would have it, he immediately stubbed his toe and went down on the floor, groaning in pain. When he was assured that nothing was broken, play resumed. Like the others, he started playing more carefully, but also smarter. He was still working his feet and legs, but he was also working his brain, attentive to the geometry of play, the opportunities to enter into the game, anticipating his next move rather than poking at the ball or whacking it blindly downfield.

Then another fortuitous moment. The same reticent kid moved into an open space, received a measured pass and scored a cracking goal, striking the ball accurately first time, the sort of move he rarely achieved during regular play. The pass had been delivered with a measured velocity that allowed him to hit the ball cleanly between the cones marking the goal line.

The kid burst into a wide grin to shouts of "How's that toe feeling now?"

The game, which had previously replicated the outdoor American game of random long balls and bunching players chasing each other, began to change into something else, into something more like "the beautiful game."

Instead of an advantage, footwear had been an impediment for these kids. The lack of protective fabric from a shoe meant that they had to kick the ball with proper technique to avoid stubbing their toes. The coach did not have to nag the players. Barefooted contact with the ball taught the lesson directly. At a minimum, kicking the ball incorrectly barefooted is painful. At a maximum, kicking the football incorrectly will result in a bloody big toenail and maybe even a broken toe. Conversely, striking the ball correctly barefooted helps achieve a level of control and soft touch that is the mark of a competent footballer.

The same lessons apply to defending. The first lesson in defending is not to clumsily poke a foot out and lunge at an attacking player. Such a move immediately places the defender at a wrong-footed disadvantage, with body momentum hurling in the direction opposite the attacker who may advance by a simple feint and dribble. A barefooted defender would not make such a mistake, exposing the toes to injury. Instead, a barefooted defender will try to anticipate the direction of the attacker's momentum, to arrive first, and to separate the attacker from the ball.

Ironically a lack of equipment, of stuff, in this case of shoes, was an advantage. What about the expensive new uniforms, warm-ups, and knapsacks that club teams encourage and even require their players to buy? Not to mention the expensive coaching and travel that is the backbone of the club financial model. Does endowing children with the outer accoutrements of high-level players, as if they were mini-professionals, develop their abilities? Or sorry kids, is it like putting lipstick on a pig?

The Blessings of Bare feet

The lesson from playing barefooted runs contrary to every assumption that Americans hold dear about success. The ruling idea is always to "build a better mousetrap." To have better and more equipment than the competition, whether in business, war, or politics. The essential lesson of American history has been whoever has better stuff wins. If a city has a brand-new school building, then education must be excellent. A city with beautiful playing fields must have good sports. Or perhaps excess stuff is like the mini-mansions that look great from the outside but are too big to keep clean and become repositories for things that do not really make us happy.

The beautiful game imparts a lesson Americans have yet to digest. This is not because the American optimistic belief in the capacity of the individual to overcome adversity and achieve success is flawed in a larger sense. The best solution to a problem is not necessarily more stuff, more equipment, or even better organization. There is an advantage in the humility to admit that in certain cases, like with the beautiful game, less-is-more.

The Shoeless Ones Rule Britannia

The beautiful game, the one the world fell in love with, as noted in chapter one, was introduced by British sailors who might have even played on the wooden decks of their ships and on the docks of ports from Genoa to Buenos Aires. Their games attracted curious and admiring spectators who wanted to play too. The footwear of British sailors at the time was much akin to wooden clogs, a hindrance to playing football. Football became the world's game when learned and played and spread in its naked essence: barefooted.

Pele, the greatest footballer of all time, learned to play barefooted. Pele's first team called themselves the "shoeless ones," because that was who they were. Their foundation in the game was in shoeless, barefooted play. In Brazil, the barefooted game has been christened *pelada* in his honor. The importance of such a testimonial in favor of barefooted soccer cannot be overestimated. Pele began his professional career in the Brazilian first division at age fifteen. At age seventeen, he scored two goals in the first of three World Cup titles he won as a player. Nobody has ever come close to achieving Pele's level of success in the game.

To this day, Americans and other nationals who might consider themselves adept at the game are stunned at the high level of ball control on the beaches and streets of Brazil. Brazilian players have an ability with the ball unattainable for someone who did not learn to play barefooted.

Kids growing up playing barefooted on the street may not necessarily become great players. Yet, anyone who learned to play barefooted gains an ability to kick the ball that does not require money or coaching. Playing barefooted teaches correct technique seamlessly. A kid who toes an inflated ball barefooted immediately realizes how not to kick a ball. No explanation required.

This begs the question of why introduction to the game for America's children is not done barefooted? The only explanation is that parts of the world, including America, suffer from a hangover of rules and practices from the late nineteenth century British gentry. Why should American children, who live in a country whose founding fathers had the courage to throw off the yoke of the British aristocracy, still be conditioned by the British Empire, which ceased truly being an empire sometime in the last century?

Maybe American children should copy Pele and have their first contact with the game be barefooted? The British

Empire won one (contested) World Cup. Pele won three with Brazil.

Earth Grounding

On occasion methods borne from necessity in simpler times prove worthy. Going barefooted as a child and even into adulthood may have physiological and psychological benefits. There is even a theory from the world of alternative medicine that physical contact between bare feet and the earth fosters a chemical reaction dubbed, "Earth grounding," held essential for human development. The theory posits that a reaction between the human body and the earth has both psychological and physical benefits and is part of the atavistic makeup of the human species.[1]

Upon first consideration, such an idea may seem like lunacy. If one reflects on human evolution, however, the idea gains legitimacy. The prehistoric ancestors of *Homo sapiens* spent most of their days walking, looking for something to eat, and running away to avoid being eaten. Philosophical theories dating from ancient Greece connect walking to clear thinking derived from this eat-or-be-eaten dialectic. Aristotle's peripatetic school championed the idea of learning by travelling from place to place on foot. The advantages of walking for thinking were touted by German philosopher Kant and the American, Henry Thoreau.

In the mid-twentieth century, a podiatrist, Simon Winkler, penned the book, *Take off Your Shoes and Walk.* Winkler became known as somewhat of a foot fanatic. He theorized that the industrialization of footwear caused diseases and maladies, both physical and psychological. Before recorded history, humans did not have readily available footwear beyond what they could fashion out of materials found in nature. Even in ancient times, footwear was quite simple, limited to leather sandals, moccasins, or boots, which at their most sophisticated, at least in ancient Roman times, had metal studs on the sole for traction.

"One Word: Plastics"

Until the introduction of plastic- and petroleum-related products in the twentieth century, football boots were made of leather, which molded naturally to the foot of the wearer. In recent times, even in the mid-twentieth century, manufactured shoes had to be "broken in," worn for a considerable time, to avoid painful blisters. Before new, stiff leather football boots were put on the foot for play, they were immersed in a tub or bucket of water until completely soaked. The wet leather molded to the shape of the wearer's foot. The practice was similar to how new, stiff denim jeans were broken in before the 1980s, before becoming available pre-washed and softened. The idea of buying expensive football boots for a child who will outgrow them after a few months did not exist outside the upper classes. For kids like Pele, of course, the entire question of what shoe to wear or buy was moot.

The latest boots from Adidas or Nike bear names like *Hypervenom, Predator*, and *Nemeziz*, more like military hardware or dinosaurs than anything you would want to put on your foot. The trend in football boots is increasingly toward artificial fabrics, which have allowed vendors to demand higher prices to cover expenses from research and development. But are these latest advances in shoe technology an improvement? If shoes hinder learning, why do kids learn to play in them?

Disintegrating Castilian Boots

A Spanish footballer reminisced about his all-time favorite pair of football boots from his childhood in the 1970s. At the time, the Spanish currency, the *peseta*, was woefully valued. The cost of a pair of West German Adidas or Pumas was out of the question for a boy who would need a new pair in a few months anyway.

One Spanish manufacturer offered shoes, which cleverly mimicked the style and markings of the Puma cleat, on a simple rubber sole. These shoes fit perfectly and became like a second skin to the player. Then he wore them in the rain and to his dismay, they disintegrated upon contact with water. Instead of leather, or even plastic, they were made of hardened painted cardboard, which when fused with the sweat from the feet of the young player had formed into the most comfortable pair of shoes he had ever worn. Those cardboard disintegrating football boots were as close as one could get to going barefooted, to being unencumbered by equipment that may be a learning impediment.

Handicap Training

To kick a ball with glistening kangaroo leather shoes is pleasurable. However, in the training and learning for any discipline, the best tools and equipment should be reserved for the technically proficient, for whom quality tools and equipment may provide advantage in competition.

There is little relative advantage to be gained by adorning someone technically inexpert with first-rate equipment. Swordsmen of past eras learned with wooden or metal rods, not fine steel blades. One does not put an inexpert rider on a thoroughbred. Anyone who cannot play the violin sounds just as awful on a Stradivarius as on a department store, plastic knockoff. There is no rationale for providing footballers who cannot strike and control the ball expertly with all six parts of the foot with the best footwear. In this case, the clothes do not make the man.

Until children can adequately kick and control a sock stuffed with rags, barefooted on the six surfaces of the foot, do kids really need fine leather cleats to say nothing of *Predators* and *Hypervenoms*? In soccer, as demonstrated by the boys in the opening anecdote to this chapter, such accoutrements hinder learning and skill development.

Not wearing shoes to learn to play soccer is a form of handicap training—not a handicap in the sense of a physical malady, but training with the imposition of deliberate obstacles to develop technique, strength, and creativity.

The ancient Roman legions reportedly trained with weapons heavier than those wielded in battle. After such a training regimen, Roman legionaries went into combat feeling light and agile, even rested despite the stress of war. The history of the ancient Roman army is replete with examples of outnumbered Romans carrying the day due to their collective technical and organizational superiority, as well as their individual ability and adaptability. When the ancient Romans were outmanned, they did not panic. Training with deliberate obstacles fostered adaptability and resilience. (Some of these ancient exploits are no longer familiar, but for fun let's cite Caesars's victory over Vercingetorix when outnumbered at the Battle of Alesia, or Suetonius's victory over Boudica when outnumbered at the Battle of Watling Street.)

Closer to home is the anecdote of a former California surfer who went to live in the Midwest and returned years later for a visit. He marveled at how the locals skipped painlessly among the sharp, craggy rocks on the surfable Southern California shoreline while he struggled, feet writhing in pain, trying to reach the waves.

Pele learned to play with the seeming handicap of being barefooted. But was this really a disadvantage? Would Pele have developed his remarkable touch and feel for the game if he had learned with the best available equipment of top-flight boots and a regulation leather ball? When he received proper equipment, like an ancient Roman soldier, playing seemed comparatively easy.

Providing children with the best equipment may elicit a pleasant reaction as a birthday or holiday gift but does little to foster their creativity, skill, and adaptability. A good soccer player must be able to kick and control the ball with each bare foot—the essence of the beautiful game. In America, the game is encumbered by unnecessarily expensive equipment that does not really help children learn to play.

So if the equipment is an obstacle to learning the game, why   use   it?

3. No Drills

Another snowy day with kids aged six to ten playing barefooted and with differently sized futsals on half a basketball court. The kids needed some stimulus, something to get to the next level. They were ready for the next step: no drills.

Their coach was still there watching play, changing things up when the game became uneven or a squabble broke out among the kids. He would switch teams, throw out a different ball, or conditions on play such as one touch, three touches, or scoring off a pass. However, the coach was not doing what Americans would define as coaching. He was mostly sitting down on the sidelines, arms folded, chatting with one of the parents. So how were the kids learning and developing into better players? The deficiencies in American play are in technical ability, speed of play, and the creativity that may be more correctly named guile or trickery. Can thinking faster and figuring out how to trick an opponent really be taught?

Shoeless Soccer (Just Add Brazilian)

The solution was simple. The coach and parents hired a Brazilian college student, not to coach the children but to play with them. This Brazilian lad's job was to play all-time offense or to join the weaker side when necessary, engaging in the sort of chatter expected at a high-level game among teammates about receiving passes, moving to space, coming back on defense.

Before the Brazilian joined their practice routine, the children had learned some moves from their American coach, who had diligently scoured the internet for examples of dribbling feints. The moves were named after famous players: the Cruyff, the Ronaldino, the Cristiano, and the Ronaldo. The coach had provided the kids' parents with internet links so they could watch and share the moves on the computer, maybe even try them together for some bonding. The coach demonstrated the moves at practice, and the children dutifully attempted mastery, standing at arm's length like a cadre of military recruits. The problem, of course, was that the coach had not grown up playing on the street where such moves are standard currency. The children's mimicry of what they saw on the computer and in practice was functional, but not natural.

This artificiality diminished when the young Brazilian, who had learned such moves as part of play rather than as part of organized practice, joined the small-sided game. His head fakes, feints, and nutmegs (what much of the world calls a *tunnel*) brought smiles to the faces of the children who began to copy him. Nutmegging became as important for the kids as scoring a goal. One kid innocently asked, "Do you know Neymar?"

The Brazilian's advice seemed pedestrian. "You cannot nutmeg someone whose legs are not apart." "You cannot score, if you do not shoot." It was like Yogi Bera's, "You can observe a lot by just watching."

The Brazilian introduced the schoolyard trick of, "What's that over there?" to get the kid playing defense to look away. The Brazilian purposely faced in the opposite direction from where he intended to pass or dribble. Such tricks are standard in pickup basketball on blacktops around the country but not at the early stages of American youth soccer.

The Brazilian juggled the ball in the air to get around a couple of kids answering the question, "Why do we have learn to juggle?" more eloquently than any lecture or explanation from the coach.

To the question of, "How can we learn to juggle like you?" He brought in a tennis ball, which he bounced on the floor and hit up once with his bare foot. Then he switched feet and began juggling with the tennis ball as if it were regulation size. The kids understood immediately: if you can juggle a tennis ball, then juggling a regulation-size ball is easy.

He then showed the kids how to retain possession of the ball by shielding, keeping the other player away by keeping one's arms down and not raising the elbow, which would attract the eye of a referee. This technique, he explained, was perfected by the great Brazilian player, Ronaldino.

The children did not have to be told to try the new moves. They were drawn instinctively to the fun in guile and trickery. The speed of play increased. The children, who naturally craved praise from someone older and more capable, wanted to be in the correct spot to either pass to the Brazilian or to receive a pass from him. They copied him, the way that kids have always copied older and better players in playground ball or street ball.

In the example above, the surrogate coach or facilitator, the Brazilian, was playing with the kids. He was one of them. Where was the coach during all this? Simple, playing bad cop. Whenever there was a reason for strife, a quibble among players, disagreement about a foul or ball possession, the coach (or director of coaching) would step in as the *voice of authority.*

In the minds of the kids, this setup established a division which aided the lessons. The surrogate coach-facilitator, who played amongst them, became the purveyor of the joy and discovery of creativity in the game. The coach or coaching director became the authority figure, a reminder of responsible behavior and mutual respect. This division enhanced the delivery of the skill lessons the surrogate coach-facilitator imparted on the field as well as the behavioral lessons from the director of coaching, playing bad cop on the sidelines.

This approach, *shoeless soccer,* is already in practice in many training sessions where a younger assistant coach aids a senior colleague. The drawback is that the surrogate coach-facilitator may become just another voice of authority, rather than one of the kids. The player may become so involved in playing that he forgets the mission to let the kids have the ball the majority of the time.

Having younger players copy an older expert player increases the fun, learning, and development of children. More importantly, the approach renders moot one of the absolute drawbacks of US soccer, which is the expense and hassle of travel to find higher-level competition. Higher-level play may be introduced by having children play with older children or with coaches who are technically and culturally proficient, like the Brazilian lad who enjoyed playing and brought smiles to the faces of those kids on that wintery day.

The *Shoeless Soccer* and the Communicative Approaches

America's well-financed amateur club teams already scour the internet and have their coaches attend seminars and conferences to learn the latest drills and practice techniques from the top youth-development academies in the world. A recent initiative of the US Club Soccer organization has been to import experts from the Spanish club system, La Liga, to conduct coaching and training seminars. The motto of the program is hopeful: "better coaches=better players."[1] Undeniably, having a better coach can help a player to improve. US clubs may vaunt the same drills as the Barcelona youth team or the German Academy. The pitfall is that best drills and preparation might become just another aspect of the less-is-more paradox. If US children lack the spontaneous and unconscious ability with the ball that is culturally indigenous in soccer-playing countries like Spain, then American kids will always be playing catch-up. Super coaching, travel, and flashy uniforms will not fix US soccer's essential deficiencies in creativity, skill, and independence learned in street soccer.

A solution for US soccer might be to pivot off indigenous attempts to improve another area in which the US is deficient: speaking foreign languages. American reticence to embrace soccer as the national sport parallels the way American culture devalued immigrants' linguistic heritage. Immigrants who landed on American shores sought to assimilate into the "melting pot" of American life. The most obvious tactic was to speak English rather than their heritage language. A common anecdote among children of immigrants in the twentieth century and before was that their parents insisted on speaking English at home because they wanted to leave the Old World behind.

Unfortunately, Americans are exceptional in the world for their monolingual tendencies. This deficiency has been noted as a disadvantage in child development. Children who speak a second tongue apparently activate more parts of their brains.[2]

Could this linguistic deficiency have an analogy in American sports culture? Does emphasis on catch-and-throw games deprive American children of exposure to the unpredictability and lack of control inherent in kick-the-ball games like soccer?

In recognition of the deficiencies in foreign-language abilities, American scholars invented a teaching method, the *communicative approach*, which was a reaction against the *grammar translation approach*, the basis for teaching the dead languages of Latin and ancient Greek. In the grammar translation approach, students memorized conjugations and vocabulary, relying on grammatical rules to discern meaning. The grammar translation approach led to ability in the subject, but not fluency. How many people who studied Latin or ancient Greek can actually conduct a conversation in those ancient tongues?[3]

The communicative approach, in contrast, introduced authentic materials and taught modern tongues as living languages. The emphasis shifted from grammar to speaking and pronunciation. Students sitting at their desks waiting to be quizzed individually by a teacher are like soccer players standing in line to kick the ball in front of a coach. In the communicative approach, the teacher welcomes the entire class to participate in target language games and activities. Teachers and students conduct interviews, play word games, and act in role-playing skits in the target language without translation into the mother tongue. The communicative approach under the guidance of an inspired and dedicated teacher can be fun, something not always equated with school. The goal of the communicative approach is to reach the spontaneous and unconscious competence that is the mark of fluency. Could this approach be applied to learning to play soccer as it has been to learning to speak a foreign language?

The Achilles heel of the communicative approach is often that the teachers are not native speakers. Their ability and pronunciation in the target language is learned, neither spontaneous nor unconsciously competent. With the communicative approach, students do learn to speak more of the target language than under the grammar translation approach. However, fluency in a foreign language eventually requires full immersion, living or studying in the country where the target language is spoken twenty-four hours a day. To achieve fluency, a student must learn to read, think, and even dream in what had previously been a foreign tongue. These spontaneous abilities cannot be learned by sitting at a desk and memorizing grammatical tables or by standing in line to perform repeated soccer drills.

A student travelling to a country where the language they have studied is the native tongue is often amazed by how fast the natives speak. Similarly, the major deficiency for American youth soccer players is the ability to play as quickly as kids who have learned playing street ball. To speed up play and to challenge American children to reach the technical levels of children in soccer-playing nations, America's youth should not wait in line to perform drills that recall the grammar translation approach of learning Latin and ancient Greek. Sending American children to foreign countries to learn to play soccer would be silly and expensive. Why not adapt the lessons of the communicative approach in foreign language education to soccer? Why not introduce what foreign language teachers call "authentic materials" into organized soccer practice and play?

Here the solution is simple, cheap, and straightforward. Introduce the speed and the authenticity of street play into soccer training through the *shoeless soccer* approach described in this chapter's opening anecdote. Children should play small-sided games (ideally 3v3), on hard surfaces, that recall street ball and schoolyard play, with differently sized balls, preferably barefoot. These games should not necessarily be under the direction of a coach imparting lectures and drills. Instead, the games should have an all-time offensive, technically and culturally proficient player who is older than the children. This surrogate coach or facilitator could be of high school or college age. Children naturally mimic youths who are not quite adults because children can imagine themselves at the next stage of their physical and mental development more readily than as fully formed adults.

This surrogate coach-facilitator must introduce an element of speed into play with solid technique, intelligent ball distribution, and above all, the trickery and guile that is the essence of the street game. This facilitator should also not dominate play, but allow the children to enjoy possession of the ball the majority of playtime.

Interventions by a senior-level director of coaching could be limited to positive suggestions for improvement that reinforce the experience from these small-sided games. Such comments may occur before or after play with examples of exercises to improve juggling, dribbling with a weak foot, or whatever technical deficiency the young players display. In this manner, the children will gain awareness of their strengths and weaknesses and realize that their coach cares about them and offers a path to improvement, an answer to the question, "How can I get better?" Parents will be satisfied that their children are aware of their progress and understand that to improve they must practice their craft and then play, play, and play some more. This is a lesson applicable to more than just soccer.

USSF Teaching Approach

One may always judge the quality of a coach or a teacher by how much time players or students wait in line for a turn to kick the ball or answer a question. Some, not all, soccer practices in the US reveal children standing in line, listening to a coach barking orders. Ultimately, in such an environment what a child really learns is how to stand in line and take orders.

USSF (United States Soccer Federation) courses teach coaches observing an error to shout, "Freeze," and then to ask players to put themselves back where they were before the mistake occurred. The "freeze" method is the ultimate form of standing in line waiting for the teacher to stop talking. The idea is that by replicating the moment of a tactical or technical mistake, players may be guided to avoid future errors. However, such artificial interventions do not foster the spontaneous, unconscious competence of fluency. Having to think of grammatical rules while speaking a foreign tongue may result in a pedestrian ability, but will be slow and artificial. Imagine trying to tell a joke while keeping in mind the grammatical rules of the punch line. Shouting, "Freeze" evokes the player's waking mind, the ego. The interruption will cause players to hesitate and overthink the next time they find themselves in a similar situation. Instead of reacting instinctively and spontaneously, a player might hesitate and ask themself, "Now, what did that coach say?"

Above, we mentioned how non-native language teachers are the Achilles heel of the communicative approach in second-language instruction. Non-native teachers may be capable of teaching the grammar and introducing authentic materials for an enjoyable and revelatory classroom experience. However, they lack the natural spontaneity of a native speaker. Similarly, coaches who grew up in the American catch-and-throw sports culture may not be entirely competent to teach technical skills or tactics in soccer. The remedy is simply to step back and stop coaching and let the game teach itself barefooted and on hard surfaces. Let the kids play, preferably with an older, more experienced player or two tossed into the mix to show (not explain) how the game is played.

The advantage of the communicative approach to language teaching is that the classroom also becomes a place where students may enjoy social interaction. Students talk to each other and even make friends while enjoying the games and skits of the communicative approach to foreign language instruction. Why not apply that same approach to soccer?

Elbow Tag?

I had declined to coach my son's team because I figured once he was eight years old, he should benefit by learning from someone else. Aristotle is credited with saying, "Give me the boy until he is seven, and I will show you the man." Aristotle taught Alexander the Great, who conquered the known world of his day, a good enough testimonial for me.

One spring practice, I observed the new coach of my son's U9 team leading an odd drill. The kids were divided into groups of four. Two of the children balanced a ball between their four elbows. They then transferred the ball to the four elbows of an awaiting pair of players. The drill was a relay race with the ball held between elbows.

Most of the kids on the team lacked basic, ball control skills. So the idea that practice time was spent on elbows looked … here one does not want to use unkind words like "stupid," but what would you call it? The absolute difference between a peek at my children's practices abroad versus those in the US, was that abroad, the coaches were uniformly ex-professionals. At practices in the US, I often wondered what was going on. The elbow relay drill seemed like something out of a corporate team-building manual.

The newly assigned coach was a player on the local university team, athletic and able with the ball. I had assumed my son would be in good hands. After practice, hands behind my back, I respectfully approached to ask about the elbow drill.

The answer was, "team building."

I had enough experience in American soccer culture to know that there was no use arguing about the elbow relay. I asked my son if perhaps he would like to try basketball or baseball. He could still play soccer abroad during the summer.

The Limits of Education

A little explanation about the word "drill." A "drill" is something that turns around on itself. The term was applied to military parading where "drilling" is the repetition of collective movements of soldiers trained to retain formation and march where ordered. The last thing an officer needs is a soldier to think for themself and to ruin the formation of the entire cohort. If the movements of an army are not coordinated, then the result is what the ancient Roman legions (before the rot of empire) did to the barbarians. "Drills"' instill physical automation and discourage individualism. Should children playing soccer perform "drills" as if they were little soldiers? Some drills can be effective as demonstrated by approaches such as the Coerver training method. However, what a child learns from a drill like the elbow relay is not foot skills, but how to obey orders. The deficiencies in US youth soccer are in individual skill and creativity, not respect for authority.

The elbow relay could be dismissed as the fruit of the imagination of a well-meaning but misguided American college kid, but this is not the case. A similar elbow-tag drill appears in *The 2015 Official US Youth Soccer Coaching Manual*, chapter 6, entitled, "Coaching Nine and Ten Year Olds: Team Identity."[4] Under the chapter title is a quote from Friedrich Frobel, a nineteenth-century German pedagogue who coined the term *kindergarten*. Frobel championed the idea of learning through play. He was a disciple of Johann Heinrich Pestalozzi, who in turn was a follower of Jean Jacques Rousseau. And here we are going to get into some trouble.

Rousseau lived just before the French Revolution in the late 1700s. He had idealistic visions about the freedom and moral rectitude of "noble savages." If he had been directing westerns, the cowboys would always have been the bad guys. (Ironically, Rousseau abandoned his own five children to orphanages, the equivalent of a death sentence at the time.) Bertrand Russell, writing during WWII, placed Rousseau at the philosophical origins of social Darwinism and totalitarianism.[5] There is no greater condemnation possible. Pivoting off Rousseau's vision of the essential goodness of people uncontaminated by the ills of society, some rulers (actually dictators) enforced political solutions to create "perfect societies." When these political solutions did not eliminate humanity's flaws, the results were the often murderous acts of fanatics who believed that "orders must be obeyed at all times." According to Russell, these horrors have roots in Rousseau's idealistic vision, regardless of whether or not that was his intention.

This is not to conflate the authors of the *US Soccer Youth Manual* with the tragedies of human history. The cultural problems facing US soccer are only partly attributable to this drive to control and transform. The true problem with the soccer manual's elbow drill is in teaching approach. The DNA of the *US Soccer Coaching Manual* has roots in the work of educational reformers like Frobel who were reacting against the old grammar translation approach in which young children memorized Latin declensions. Nineteenth-century educational reformers recognized that children also learned by tapping into their natural instinct to play. The elbow-relay drill would seem to have been invented as a means to introduce children to concepts and teamwork by separating them from the rigors of "oppressive" source material. However, playing soccer should not be "oppressive." Playing ball is not like memorizing Latin or ancient Greek cases under the threat of being whacked by a stern nineteenth-century taskmaster. Soccer taps into the natural play instincts of a child. Soccer is a fun game. The deficiencies in American soccer are the lack of individual skill and creativity. These deficiencies can be redressed by increasing the amount of time children play in settings that approximate the chaos and freedom of street soccer, of play, as closely as possible. How many times have you seen two players balancing the ball between their elbows in a game?

Education is no cure-all. Edward Gibbon, the historian, commented on how the evil Roman emperor Commodus, depicted in the film *Gladiator*, turned out so poorly despite being raised by his father, the stoic philosopher, Marcus Aurelius. Gibbon explained, "The power of instruction is seldom of much efficacy except in those happy dispositions where it is almost superfluous."[6] In other words, you cannot teach someone who does not want to learn or is physically incapable of learning.

Marcus Aurelius had Commodus educated by the highest classical standards. But Commodus's disposition led him to reign like the John Belushi character from the film *Animal House* rather than like his stoic father. Commodus ignored the problems of the Empire, partied, and pretended he was a gladiator, until his guards tired of the game and killed him.

If the target for education cannot receive the lessons of instruction, then, as Gibbon warned, education is "seldom of much efficacy." If American children lack basic, spontaneous, familiarity with the ball, then coaching, training, or education can achieve only limited results.

In education, as in soccer, the United States suffers from the less-is-more/more-is-less paradox. The United States currently confuses education with education budgeting, as if the path to a better education were newer buildings, more computers, or "smart boards" (whatever those are), more bureaucracy, and more administration rather than what students ingest from their lessons. The United States spends as much if not more per student on education than any country in the world. Yet, the educational achievement levels of American students are nowhere near the world's best. More is not necessarily better. There is a clear parallel to soccer education and the money parents spend for their children to become skilled players, as if the keys to better US soccer were super-prepared coaches, drills, fancy uniforms, pristine fields, cleats, and distant tournaments. Ironically, American kids actually participate in more organized soccer games than their counterparts abroad.[7] Evidently quality of play and practice is more important than quantity.

The key to improving US soccer is to foster learning environments that approximate the conditions of the unstructured play of street ball. This approach is in tune with the foundations of sports psychology. Over awareness and concentration cause the body to underperform due to the distraction from the ego, the waking mind.[8] What better way to encourage children to overthink than having a coach yell, "Freeze!" whenever they make a tactical boo-boo? When the basic football skills of American children become unconscious, as spontaneous as opening a door, putting on pants, or brushing teeth, then American children will be able to receive the lessons of higher-level coaching. Then, the American game will have a chance to compete at an international level and American children will not seem out of place in fancy uniforms.

4. No Balls

The greatest footballer of all time, Pele, grew up in a family that could not afford a ball. To placate his son, Pele's father put rags in a sock for a makeshift ball. Anything from Pele's soccer life, as in the *Lives of the Saints* in parochial education, is a source for precedent and inspiration. The ball anecdote is no exception.

American kids do not need to throw away their Adidas World Cup replica balls and replace them with some rags in a sock because of this Pele story. Yet, the very last thing a child needs in order to learn to play the game is a regulation, size 5 ball. With balls, the key is variety rather than quality or quantity.

Montessori Balls

For a three-year-old, making a ball out of some rags and an old sock is a lesson about exploring the world and solving problems through creativity. This recalls the Montessori teaching approach.[1] A product of a child's creativity is automatically friendly and familiar.

Could American children who grow up with catch-and-throw games like American football, basketball, and baseball have a first introduction to soccer with a homemade ball, like Pele's? After making the ball, children could be introduced to the fundamental rule of the game because the ball is for kicking, no hands. Each child could kick the "ball," hopefully barefooted, into goals set around a room. There could be rewards of applause for scoring a goal, maybe even a goal celebration dance like Vincenzo Montella's joyful airplane pantomime or Cristiano Ronaldo's Superman flex, although Montella's romp is probably easier to communicate to three-year-old boys and girls.

After rag-sock balls, other balls of different size and density, whether plastic bottles or tennis balls, could be introduced so children may recognize the relationship between how they kick an object and what happens to it. A competent footballer should be able to control a tennis ball as well as a regulation-size football.

The presumption of a consumerist society is that better equipment confers superior ability, just like a fancier car or bigger house communicates higher social status and wealth. Parents may be taken aback when they realize that children who learn to play with socks full of rags become better players than their own progeny who can vaunt the latest FIFA-approved, synthetic, World Cup replica ball. Like learning barefooted rather than in shoes or on a small sandlot rather than a muddy, high-grass field, a seeming handicap due to a lack of equipment can be an advantage.

Less-Is-More

As with shoes, balls present a potential problem. If too many real footballs are introduced too soon, excess reduces perception of value. Children, like adults, are attracted to objects that are rare or that inspire the wonder and awe of others because they are perceived to be special. For children with the economic means to acquire as many balls as they might desire, abundance decreases value and interest. A child with only one football is more likely to prize it than dozens of forgotten footballs strewn about the house or abandoned in the yard. Maradona's joy at his first football is illustrative. Maradona, like Pele, learned to play with makeshift balls or the balls of other children. When Maradona finally received a ball of his own, he treasured that ball as a trusted friend that would always be there to play with him and would never abandon him. That ball is now the stuff of literature and legend in Maradona's home country of Argentina. Everybody there knows the role it played in the making of an exceptional player.

Variety Is the Spice of Soccer Balls

The lesson with balls is that variety trumps quality or expense. Differently sized balls impart different technical lessons. To dribble a ball made of rags, the best technique is to jab at each stride with the outside of the foot near the pinky toe. This approach is also effective when sprinting with a regulation-size ball and may seem to come naturally to Brazilians, but only because they play with differently sized balls, with futsal or *futebol de salão* balls, or in the case of Pele, with rags in a sock.

Europeans, particularly northern Europeans and the British, historically learned to play with adult, size 5 balls. They are not naturally any less capable nor talented than kids in Brazil. However, they are at a disadvantage with respect to Brazilian players, who learn the techniques required to play with balls of different size, weight, consistency, and inflation.

Differences in inflation change technique. Controlling an overinflated ball is difficult and can even be painful, particularly if hit incorrectly barefooted. In contrast, a deflated ball is easier to control and may aid a player who is first learning to dribble and juggle. Referees will replace deflated balls in both recreational and professional football because deflated balls slow down the game.

Spaniards are renowned for training with hyperinflated balls. This is a variation of the previously mentioned ancient Roman army practice of using weapons heavier in training than those wielded in battle. A Spanish player accustomed to practicing with a hyperinflated ball has an immediate advantage when controlling a standard regulation, non-hyperinflated ball. A technically proficient player will be able to shift seamlessly from play from a hyperinflated ball to a standard inflated ball or from a regulation, FIFA size 5 ball to a tennis ball.

With a very small ball, like a tennis ball, the natural solution is to stop the ball with the sole of the foot, almost stepping on the ball to bring it to a complete halt. This technique is familiar to Brazilians and is standard practice in the *futebol de salão* indoor court game, played with a non-bounce, size 2 ball. Or in the case of futsal, the indoor court game that is played with a non-bounce, size 3 or 4 ball.

The idea to control the ball with the sole of the foot or to dribble by poking the ball at each stride with the pinky toe will not occur naturally to players who learn to play with an adult, regulation FIFA, size 5 football on high grass. A large football, particularly on high grass, will roll perfectly well after a quick jab with the toe. This unfortunately prevents the player from fully developing the touch attainable via some handicap training with differently sized and differently inflated balls.

He's Not Heavy, He's My Soccer Ball

The theory goes that in ancient times, football was a gruesome victory revelry of an army or marauding band, which shoved the decapitated head of a vanquished foe into a sack to be kicked around the camp by partying soldiers. Polo apparently has similar grisly origins, except soldiers were on horseback prodding the ball/bag with lances. Since those barbaric origins, the weight of the football has determined the course of the development of the game.

The hand-stitched, thick leather balls prior to the 1970 World Cup were permeable, heavy, irregular objects with patches of leather rather than uniform surfaces. A pre-1970 ball, soaked in water, could knock even the most resilient heavyweight boxer unconscious if delivered with pace. Johan Cruyff, the great Dutch player, remarked that when he started playing for the professional club Ajax at age fifteen, he could hardly kick the ball twenty meters and certainly had no chance of placing it into the upper corner of a goal from distance. The heavy ball determined the speed of the game and required physical strength. The ability to kick the heavy ball a great distance afforded a tactical advantage and became a central aspect of the nineteenth-century English kick-and-chase style with players tearing down the wings and crossing the heavy ball for a beefy and ruthless center forward to smash into the back of the net.

Since the 1970s, the official FIFA ball has become lighter and lighter, favoring the Brazilian *jogo bonito,* Catalan *tiki taka*, and Dutch total football schools that prize technique over physicality. To strike the pre-1970 heavy ball first-time with the foot requires a player to be well grounded, firmly placed on the feet. The heavy ball would negate the acrobatic leaps that are the delight of the *tiki taka* style. The reduction of ball weight was fundamental to that style and the FC Barcelona championship and Spanish World Cup victory that relied on it. The world-champion Spanish team would not have been able to pass the pre-1970 ball with their characteristic, dizzying series of first-time touches.

Women have taken advantage of changes in ball weight to develop a female tradition. Lighter female body weight and lesser physical strength compared to males are no longer impediments. A lighter ball allows passing and shooting in the same manner as adult males. The decrease in ball weight may also explain Italy's decline in recent international competition, as lighter balls provide an advantage to attacking players, negating Italy's tradition in defensive play.

At this point we may appear to be digressing. What does a discourse on the history and geography of soccer balls have to do with kids playing better soccer? The point here is simple, almost painfully so. Soccer is a game played with a ball. Full stop. Yes, at a certain level and in certain high-stakes competitions, official size and weight matter.

But from tennis balls to bundles of rags, from water-logged leather to high tech Jabulanis, the game can be played and is played. Great players will be the ones who can kick and control any of these spherical objects, anywhere, anytime, and on any surface. We fret about the wrong things in US soccer. And our players suffer.

Super Tele Balls

A man who had grown up playing football in Italy had two sons with whom he wanted to share his love for the game. The first son went through the recreation, club-travel, and ODP (Olympic Development Program) system during his school year in the States. In the summers, he would accompany the family to Italy, where he would play with Italian kids at the *scuola calcio* soccer camps, more like day-care centers than the serious soccer-training schools the name implies.

Every summer, the son arrived in Italy at a disadvantage compared to Italian kids. But over the course of the summer, he improved. By summer's end, he could play with the Italian kids, and he made life-long friendships. When the family returned to the States in the fall, the son's skills and abilities declined to the level of the American kids with whom he played.

The father did not want his second child to experience the same lag, between summers and school year, which had hampered the elder sibling. Despite not having an English accent, he decided to get a USSF coaching license and offer his services to the local parks and rec department and soccer clubs. His first idea was to do something about the balls Americans used to learn the game.

He remembered his own Super Tele rubber ball from the 70s, still available at every open-air market on the Italian peninsula. The Super Tele balls are reduced in size, light and lose a bit of air daily. Children strike these balls without hesitation and develop a crisp shot. They are also easy to juggle because the ball adjusts to the level of force with which it is struck and has the predictable trajectory of a regulation size, leather ball. These qualities help a young player develop the technical accuracy which has been a trademark of Italian footballers.

American parents who put their children through the rigors of soccer practice, after soccer practice and the expense and time sink of travel soccer marvel at how non-Americans, even children, strike the ball forcefully without fear and with the sort of follow-through that is the envy of every soccer coach. In Italy, this natural, spontaneous ability with the ball derives partly from learning to play with the rubber balls like the Super Tele.

Upon returning to the States, the father ordered some online. He took his coaching license to the local parks and rec director and volunteered to lead kids like his youngest, aged four to five, in a football clinic.

On the first day, he presented the children with a roomful of inflated Super Tele balls. He asked them to remove their shoes and invited them to play. The only restriction was that they could not touch the balls with their hands.

He expected the children to start kicking and chasing the balls. Had he provided kids in Italy with the same opportunity, the room would have erupted into a chaotic kicking of balls. But nothing happened. The kids looked at the balls. Then they looked at him and awaited orders. Then they looked at their parents on the side of the gym floor for guidance. Some ran over to their mothers. The kids had no idea what to do.

The parks and rec director intervened after a few sessions and relieved the man, replacing him with local high school players who could not play soccer but knew how to make kids stand in line and await their turn to kick a ball incorrectly in their shoes. The director explained that the parents had paid for a clinic with drills and organization. One could not expect kids to just play. They had to be told what to do.

The American kids, unlike most kids around the world, had not been encouraged to kick a ball during playtime. American sports football, baseball, and basketball are catch-and-throw games. Soccer is a kick-the-ball game. In most parts of the world, the first game a child will play with a parent or a playmate after the put-everything-in-the-mouth stage, is kick-the-ball. The result is that even children who have no pretense of playing the game at a higher level, have a basic introduction as very small children and develop an attitude about kicking a ball akin to spontaneous acts like lifting a hand to wave hello. The American kids could not react like Italian kids to the Super Tele balls because by age four or five they had not kicked a ball a couple of hundred or even a couple of thousand times like kids in soccer-playing nations.

The solution here is straightforward and costs just about nothing. American parents blessed with a two-or three-year-old may offer their child a little ball with encouragement to kick it.

That's it. No lectures. No explanations. No travel out of state to toddler kick-the-ball tournaments. No need to adorn them in fancy kick-the-ball uniforms. Just playtime where our children kick a ball—any ball. And on any surface, in any space. If organization is needed, setting this up is a thing any community parks and rec program can do. So long as they understand that this is really the only thing that matters. Provide a space, toss out a ball, invite an older player or two along to show them (not tell them) how it's done. Then sit back and enjoy.

Then, when they do at last connect foot to ball, reward the children with a big smile and the utterance of something like a simple "Yes!" Nothing more. And certainly not "Good job." Playing in the US youth soccer club, pay-to-play travel system may seem like a "job," but kicking a ball should not be.

5. No Shin Guards

Sometime back in the early 1990s, a Scandinavian public-service announcement featured a couple riding a motorcycle along a country highway buck naked. While the image of two disrobed riders certainly grabbed the public's attention, the message of the ad was at least as powerful. Ride like there's nothing between you and the road. Just you with your utterly exposed, soft, naked flesh dashing full speed down the road while a matter of inches away the merciless, rock-hard asphalt rushes past at sixty-five miles per hour...

If that were you, how would you ride?

The Inanimate:

Of all the obvious differences between soccer practices in the rest of the world and their US equivalents, perhaps the most frightening for American helicopter parents is the utter absence of shin guards. Where we have observed, in Argentina, in Spain, in Italy, no one wears them in practice. Ever.

How can this be, think the parents who know that even their toddler wouldn't be allowed on most American soccer fields without massive plastic protection strapped to their chubby little legs. From their first practice at age three, children are expected to arrive with proper cleats, their own ball, a water bottle, and shin guards, which are typically on that first day all shiny, new, and adorably oversized. No guards, no play. It's common sense. Soccer is a kicking game. You try to kick the ball, you inevitably are going to get a leg. A piece or the whole thing. It's gonna happen. It's a package deal. And, of course, getting kicked in the shins really, really hurts. So, wear shin guards.

Then kick away...

The first time I noted the lack of guards overseas, I returned to my home club eager to share my observations. "Hey, Director of Coaching," I said, "Did you know that no one in Spain ever trains in shin guards?" He did not. He was mildly intrigued. We discussed the possible reasons, the benefits, and the dangers. Ultimately, though, he nixed the idea. Parents would never go for it. We'd have too many injuries. Just not worth the risks.

So how do they handle the risks in Spain I wondered? What do they do there, (besides win the World Cup…) I thought, as I walked away.

So I tabled the idea. At least for a while. Yet the more I pondered on what I'd seen, the more intrigued I became. Perhaps if we began with a younger group, with parents who didn't know "any better" and with kids who hadn't spent years already training in shin guards, we might be able to pull it off.

This past fall I had my opportunity. A very busy schedule meant I wouldn't have much time to coach. I considered skipping the fall season entirely. When several parents approached me to consider coaching their group of eight- and-nine-year-old boys, I reconsidered, realizing I might use their request as leverage to tinker a bit, to get them thinking—and their kids playing—outside the box. The parents were a fairly bright group with at least one parent having observed the same no-shin-guard practice in action regularly on frequent trips abroad. So in a preseason parents meeting, I explained the new policy, including providing some of the international context from which the idea sprang. They all agreed.

Even so, on our first day of practice every kid but two showed up wearing the protective plastic. Apparently it was fine with the parents if the rest of the boys wanted to remove their plastic body armor, but they weren't about to leave their own kid's shins exposed; no way.

Still, I decided to take what they had given. After all, you've got to begin somewhere. So we gathered the boys together, we observed the exposed shins of the two boys who had complied, and we discussed how they would feel if we kicked without control, if we went in for hard tackles. We agreed we would need to be a bit more careful today. At the end of the conversation, several other boys, though not all, voluntarily removed their own guards. And we started to play.

Thanks to the conversation, the boys began a series of mini scrimmages with that wee bit more control we had talked about. Still, less than five minutes in, one of our more reckless kids went full-tackle into one of his teammates. Ouch! Luckily no one was badly hurt. Even more luckily, the reckless one had suffered the lion's share of the pain. As the child lay there writhing on the ground, all we needed to add at that point was a, "See?" The tackles and their consequences spoke for themselves.

As one would expect, practice cleaned up immediately. Instead of engaging in a physical affair of hard, reckless kicks, our defenders began more carefully timing their challenges. On offense, players began employing more evasive strategies, adding more feints and fakes to their game, rather than simply charging full steam ahead into the scrum.

After nine months without shin guards, we've never had to insist again. No one wears them any longer. As expected, no one has been hurt any more than when they used to wear them. Better still, the game they now play more closely resembles the game played in the rest of the world. Technique, agility, and intelligence rule the day. Strength, raw speed, and reckless play have disappeared from our practices, not due to any extra effort on my part, but because such play simply is no longer worth it. It hurts. Plain and simple.

Plain and simple, indeed. These are not complicated notions. When we simplify the game, when we tear off the equipment, when we let the grass die, when we stop worrying about perfect pitches, when we jettison invasive coaching or even stop worrying about the official size, weight, and absolute perfection of the ball, the game teaches itself. Shin guards are a small matter. Their removal probably doesn't have the same immediate technical impact on the game as changing the surface we play on or removing our shoes. Barefooted kicking or play on hard surfaces immediately change the way a kid touches the ball. Not so taking off shin guards.

However, removal of such simple safeties may begin to change the way a kid *sees* the game. Play immediately becomes more about the spaces on the field, about getting yourself and the ball where the defenders are not, lest those defenders mete out real pain. Ball movement—the quicker the better—becomes key because, as the players soon discover, the longer the ball sits idly at my feet, the more likely I am to get kicked in the shins. Mindless, technically incompetent ball hogging is quickly rooted out. If, on the other hand, a kid wants to hold on to the ball—and some thankfully do—they'll need to develop an arsenal of fakes and feints lest their bare legs become a mélange of black and blue. Again, these are skills, aptitudes, and attitudes that the coach no longer needs to teach. As with the elimination of other officially "necessary" equipment, the removal of guards allows the game itself to become the teacher.

But why stop there? We've removed the grass, we've removed the shoes, and now we've removed the shin guards. We've unleashed the bare feet and the bare legs. We've reestablished our relationship with the street, the playground, and the plaza. Is there anything else, beyond our shins, begging to be free? Anything come to mind?

The Animate:

How about…the players?

Several years ago a family was arrested in Silver Spring, Maryland, for allowing their kids, ages six and ten, to walk home unaccompanied from a park. A debate played out in the media for the next couple of weeks over whether the parents were criminals or geniuses, negligent or empowering. They and others began using the term "free-range parenting" to describe their approach to raising kids. Too many restrictions, they argued, had made today's kids a dull, overweight, bored, and boorish lot. Set them free and watch them fly, they claimed. Less would be more as the kids themselves learned to make their own snacks, do their own laundry, or simply walk home from the park.

Can the same apply on a youth football field? How would you create "free-range footballers"?

If removing shin guards ain't rocket science, the answer here is even less so. After all, "free-range children" is just a fancy name for letting kids be what they had been for generations. Free to roam. A free-range footballer would simply be a kid playing a game with as few "protections" as possible. As we've discussed in previous chapters, some of the most basic of the protections are well-manicured lawns and perfectly weighted, extra-cushioned balls. Removing the shin guards is the next-level of emancipation. Daring stuff, to be sure.

But what would truly liberate the kids, make them truly "free-range" is what got the parents of the original "free-range children" in trouble: getting rid of the adults. Yes, the adults. The coaches, the referees, even the parents. Gone.

Obviously "gone" can't be literal, or at least not a hundred percent. We may be proposing a radical rethinking of soccer in the US, but radically restructuring American culture is another slightly larger ball o' wax. So, let's concede from the start that if kids are going to get together to play just about anything these days, they'll likely need an adult around. Perhaps several.

Now that we've gotten that out of the way, let's focus on the process of eliminations.

First, the coaches. No more coaches. And we'll leave it at that. Or at least pass the buck to the entire chapter we devote to it. Yes, it's stuff for an entire chapter. After all, they're the coaches. Don't we want coaches? (No. At least not the way most of us understand them).

Second, the parents. We love you. Your kid loves you. We're parents ourselves. But please, for the sake of your kid and US Soccer, disappear. Yes, you. But not because we don't like you. In fact, we like you so much, we've given you your own chapter as well.

So who else is left on the field? Ah, yes, the referees.

What is a referee? An enforcer of rules, you answer, a facilitator of smooth play. A referee is the man or woman who keeps the peace, who tells us when and where the ball went out of play and who last touched it, not to mention who broke the rules and used their hands, or even worse, broke the rules and hurt my kid, or worst of all, broke the rules and caused my kid's team (our team!) to lose.

Ah, how we need those refs.

Except, we don't. Remember all the fun pickup games we played as kids without a referee or any kind of third-party judge to make calls for us? Remember all those warm memories of self-regulated play as children, interspersed with occasional, when not frequent, spats if not all-out brawls with our friends? Those pickups may have ended with everyone storming off the field resolved to never see each other again, but the next day they produced yet another game at the same time and same place and eventually turned our punching partners into lifelong friends.

Leaving aside all that, let's just talk about the game as played today. For the sake of argument, imagine a game with all the other conditions we claim to be equally unnecessary still in place. The pitch is perfectly groomed, painted with all the right lines, and corner flags. The regulation goals are firmly affixed in place, and an officially sanctioned, properly inflated, correctly sized game ball sits in the middle of the field. Over that ball stand two opposing teams tricked out in shiny new kits, wearing the latest Nike, Adidas, and Puma footwear, and of course, all well protected in shin guards, prepared to do battle. Oh, and did we mention this was travel soccer; none of the kids from team one know anyone from team two. Everything is in place.

Except there are no referees. Imagine.

Yes, we know, all hell would break lose. No one would agree on who kicked the ball out of bounds. Or who fouled whom. Or if that goal was really scored. We'd have more hands of God on display than the Sistine Chapel viewed via kaleidoscope.

Except, of course, we wouldn't.

How do we know? Because we've seen it. Perhaps you have too. Though few and far between, occasionally local travel clubs will arrange friendlies with other clubs. Occasionally, at some of those friendlies they'll just let the kids play. Everything else looks the same. Except there's no referee. Not a single one, to say nothing of the typical team of three that dutifully keep the peace at every official game played by kids aged eleven and up.

So how does the referee-free game flow? How are throw-ins decided? How are penalties awarded? Well, the same way they were when we were kids on the playground or as they are today when, as adults, we find ourselves at the local YMCA shooting hoops with a bunch of total strangers. We figure things out. As do they. Amazing, but true.

Not only do the kids figure things out, the kids also end up playing much more loosely. In the absence of adult authority figures, the game becomes theirs. They're responsible. They can't lose their cool and expect someone else to sort things out for them. They can't lie, cheat, and steal their way to victory hoping an out-of-position ref might bail them out. It's just them and the opposition, and the two of them know who just kicked that ball out of bounds. Moreover, they both know that the other knows, and that they know the other knows that they know. So they figure things out. Or there will be no game. Their choice. After a couple of aborted matches, they'll get the picture. We all do.

But equally important to being responsible for themselves, they're no longer responsible to anyone else. There's no longer that all-powerful judge constantly looking over their shoulders. There's no longer that man or woman taking up space on the field, reminding them that they're under continuous surveillance. No one is there imposing a punitive tone and making the game seem more important than it is. Without the referee, the game remains just a game. The kids play more freely, liberated to engage with peers who, just like them, at the end of the day are going to go back home to their Pokemon cards and Power Rangers.

And did we mention how many calls even the best refs miss?

Who knows best how much the ref gets wrong? The players, of course. Moreover, with that knowledge, they can't help but play frustrated, angry, and tight. In too many cases, as we well know, their play may become increasingly violent, as they vent their frustrations, not on the ref (because, of course, the referee literally holds all the cards), but on the other team. Thus the violence escalates.

Does this mean that referees are never necessary? Of course not. Some games at higher levels do become more high-stakes. At a certain point, people begin to play for more. But how many games at the U6 through U14 level really matter? And if they so "matter" (a tournament, a championship game, etc.), what does that even mean? How serious can a game played between two groups of kids be? Especially if our endgame isn't winning or losing, but player development?

Pain and Suffering

Speaking of violence, before we conclude this rather dangerous chapter, a word on pain. After all, soccer is a game with lots of it. Soccer, like everybody, in the words of Michael Stipe, hurts. Sometimes. But thankfully, at the youth level soccer is also a game with few serious injuries. To be sure, concussions and an occasional broken arm and twisted ankle do happen. Concussions, of course, are matters of real concern. US Soccer appears to be addressing it using the best medical advice available to date. But the pain? Again, that's another story. One we need to deal with. In US youth soccer. Today.

So here we go. First, let's be clear: getting kicked in the legs by the hard-swung leg of an opponent hurts. It really, really does. Legs are powerful things. They deliver pain. But at the same time... did we mention that legs are powerful things? That means they can absorb a lot of pain as well. Anyone who has ever played more than a game or two of competitive soccer knows what we mean. Getting kicked hurts. Really, really hurts. But after a few seconds to a minute or so of writhing about on the ground, ninety-nine percent of the time you pop right up and keep playing. Perhaps the next day you'll have a bruise (though most of the time you won't even have so much as a mark to write home about). Just the memory will remain—plus the fish tale for your friends—of that excruciating, bleak moment when you thought you'd never walk again. But you'll also have the memory of when you hopped up as soon as that pass came skidding back across the field toward you, of how you continued on the rest of the evening as if nothing had happened.

Yes, that is what typically happens in football. And our kids would probably be better off understanding that fact sooner rather than later. In US youth soccer these days, we have developed a tradition of rushing onto the field the moment a player goes down. We've been there ourselves. These days it's expected. Indeed, if we don't, we're terrified some irate soccer dad or mom (we've been there ourselves) is going to rush the field and throttle us. So, instead, everyone on the field takes a knee—the ritual worship of injury—as we run out at full speed and, unfortunately, in too many cases actually carry the kid off the field (the crowning *Pieta* moment of the religiously tinged affair). As we all know, ninety-nine percent of the time that same kid somewhere between thirty seconds and five minutes later is either gleefully hopping around on the team bench or begging to be allowed back into the game. We applied no stitches, no splint, and no salve. The pain just disappeared. (A miracle!) But first we had to carry him off the field...

(Let us reiterate, once more, that we ourselves have been there as parents. It's natural for all of us to feel this way. We don't intend here to mock the natural, and at times, very necessary protective instincts of parents. Our point is to remind ourselves of something we all once understood when we were children ourselves, playing sports with our friends: sports involve pain but almost every time you get over it and move on.)

Just as in the case of losing the shin guards, the sooner our kids learn to manage their own small soccer pains, the better off they'll be. To be sure, some of this is about helping kids learn to deal with the pain of sports. But as they take some personal responsibility for that pain, their game will change. Once the coddling stops, the kids who like to be ambulanced off the field will just learn to keep playing. They'll see that going down in a crumpled heap only hurts their teammates and doesn't win an ounce of sympathy from coaches or parents. The rewards of the crash will vanish. Perhaps, as when they ditched the shin guards, they'll think differently from then on about space and ball movement, not to mention their own personal movement. Certainly they'll learn that this game is theirs. Theirs to figure out and theirs to deal with.

Naked Football:

Naked motorcyclists are terribly vulnerable. But naked motorcyclists know this. Thus they learn to ride. They ride well. Very well. They understand the technology they ride. They know the rules of the road. They pay serious attention to everything going on around them. Naked motorcyclists are better motorcyclists. Someday we may wish—or need—a motorcyclist or two to ride dangerously fast, to deliver a package in a terrible hurry, to traverse a winding, slick road at breakneck speed to save a life, or perhaps simply to do so for our viewing pleasure. At those moments, throwing a helmet and specialized protective clothing on our rider will be a simple matter. But we can be assured after years of watching them ride naked, that we're throwing that specialized gear on someone who has learned to ride right.

The analogy is obvious. The time and place will come for outstanding footballers to perform on pristine pitches, wearing the best gear, regulated by professional referees, directed by win-at-all-costs coaching staffs, while being cheered and jeered by hundreds of thousands of fans. But when that day comes, we want players who have learned to play in the most adverse conditions and who have had to figure the game out for themselves, players who are mature and resourceful, endlessly clever and effortlessly skilled, players who have honed their game in an almost limitless variety of circumstances.

Right now, US youth soccer doesn't come remotely close to that. While remaking the entire system is beyond the pay grade or know-how of most of us, simple tweaks can free up our kids. With the smallest, simplest of changes our kids can almost immediately be playing a different kind of game from what nearly everyone is currently playing in this country. One of those easiest of fixes involves simply removing all the game's special protections.

Shin guards, referees, even obsessive attention to injuries send the message to young players that playing without all the stuff is simply too dangerous. Ironically, once the stuff is on and the rest of the protections in place, the kids are encouraged to play even more recklessly, and often more dishonestly, than before. Either way, quality soccer is not served. Our children are not served.

What are the potential costs of such changes? As we've seen with shin guard removal, and as the rest of the world has been showing since the advent of the game, there are none. There are only benefits. It's that simple.

But what about ignoring the minor injuries? It's hard to see a single cost.

Finally, what about the elimination of the refs, at least from all games played up until the junior high school years? Really, what would be the cost? Maybe our kids wouldn't experience sufficient development so as to qualify for recruitment to the Premiership or La Liga or Serie A or the Bundesliga. Maybe the US wouldn't develop players who could merely earn a tie against Trinidad and Tobago to qualify for the World Cup.

Wait a minute…

Our point exactly. So what do we have to lose?

Nothing, of course. There is—how many times need we repeat—no point in continuing down the same path. We can wait for the USSF to change everything from above. Or we can begin right now by simply rethinking the way we organize the game for our kids. Rip off the shin guards, stop running out on the field for every nick and bump, and give the refs a day off. Adults need to focus on creating the closest thing to *game*-like conditions for our kids, ensuring that the game is played as a game. Set it up simple. Then get out of the way.

6. No Space

The Infinitely Elusive (and Surprisingly Destructive) Quest for the Perfect Soccer Space and the Solution Right under Your Nose

Let's return once more to the pitch itself. As we noted in "No Grass," until we address the most basic conditions of the game, such as the very surface we're playing on, everything else will be like spitting in the wind. Currently US youth soccer spends an inordinate amount of time trying to coach our way out of the very conditions we believe necessary to play the game.

So before we continue addressing how we play, we need to make sure we've clearly and thoroughly addressed the question of the where we play. Keeping that in mind, we present what could be seen as part two of "No Grass." From the question of perfect lawns we now move on to the question of the soccer space itself. Before we begin, we should probably consider once more the question of the perfect, or at least the ideal. What is the ideal space for football? What about for great football? And finally, for great football development? Now, for some anecdotes.

The Best Teammate is a Mexican Flower Pot

About a decade ago I found myself enjoying the sun on the balcony of a shelter for homeless boys during a half-hour work break. Below me a football match quickly organized itself. The game pit the local boys, ranging in age from fourteen to early adult, against the group of visiting US university students. The US students had some talent, most of them having played some organized soccer in their youth. One particularly skilled kid had spent his adolescence with one of our regional super clubs. The local boys, on the other hand, were all kids living on the streets. Given their conditions, it's unlikely any of them had ever played organized soccer, let alone anything comparable to all the club bells and whistles the one university student had been bred on.

When the game ended, my visiting college students had been thoroughly schooled. The street boys had their way. Yes, the US club player had made some nice moves and scored several admirable goals. But all in all, the local kids cleaned the visitors' clocks.

Truth is, the visitors probably never had a chance. Not because the locals were so much better, though they were. And certainly not because the local kids were faster, smarter, or better trained, because they weren't. No, the visitors had no chance because those Midwest American kids were playing on easily the strangest pitch they'd ever seen.

What was the pitch like? Well, there was a goal at one end and another at the opposite. The field was somewhat rectangular in shape, narrower in width than in length and with arguably (a minimum of) four identifiable corners. Otherwise, the pitch was about as unusual a playing space as you could imagine. Its core was really nothing more than a slightly wider-than-average driveway. That driveway, once you got beyond the length of what would be a single car, began to be chopped up on the far side of my balcony by concrete planters—really oversized flowerpots—about three feet tall and five feet square placed every five feet or so along the pitch. These pots were growing a variety of fully mature trees. On the nearside, just under my balcony was a narrow walkway, about six inches above the level of the driveway. The path was occasionally broken up by a second step or two for pedestrians to enter the building, providing the pitch a nearside border. Then, somewhere about two thirds down the pitch, there was a general dip and another planter marking the end of the official driveway, but not of the patio. There the game continued for another twenty-or-so feet of unbroken space to where the defending team's goal stood.

At one point, I was invited to come down and join the game. Looking at that space with all its obstacles, additional corners, and varied levels, and considering my relatively old age, I decided to skip this one. Instead, I stood on that balcony marveling at the strange and occasionally spectacular skills displayed by these local street kids: the turns, spins, passes, and shots to navigate around such an unusual and seemingly impossible area. I marveled even more at what they did to avail themselves of those very obstacles, the shifts in level, and the narrowing and widening of shape, to confuse the opposition and to pass the ball with speed and power from teammate to teammate.

There were moves I saw that day that I have never seen again and probably never will see again. Moves not developed on perfect football pitches but on a crazily flawed field. Moves born not out of hours of practice but out of playful necessity, the original mother of invention. For some kids this patio was perhaps the safest place in the city to play the game they loved. Yet the conditions were about as far from ideal as one can imagine and from what we would consider proper soccer. The boys simply wanted to play. So they figured things out. What they figured out looked like genius.

So were they playing what we in the USA would call good soccer?

That was precisely the question I discussed with the college students that afternoon. We decided quickly that while the kids were amazing, if we were to replay the same match on a normal grass pitch right then and there, the street kids probably wouldn't stand a chance. Their skills were brilliant but terribly limited, to say nothing of the question of the tactics and fitness that "true" soccer would demand.

But, we then pondered, what if we took them with all their crazy skills and gave them a few months or perhaps simply a few weeks to prepare? What if we gave them a chance to get just a few tactical pointers from an experienced coach, so they would get in the shape necessary to run on a traditional field? What if we gave them a month or two to eat three proper meals a day with a regular good night's rest? In contrast, what if during those same months we attempted to teach the US university students the tricks and skills of the locals? Who, when we blew that opening whistle of the hypothetical rematch on the more traditional soccer pitch, would win?

The Modern Art of Urban Football

One afternoon while heading toward Madrid's Atocha train station on my way home from work, I decided to detour across the plaza of Spain's world-famous museum of modern art, the Reina Sofía, which was more crowded than usual. I didn't typically pass through there during that late-afternoon hour, and what I saw was the perfect crowd storm. There were kids out of school for the evening, locals passing through on their evening stroll, and tourists pouring out of the museum at closing time and heading across the plaza to take their places on the nearby terraces of Spain's open-air bars and cafes. In the midst of so large a crowd what stopped me in my tracks, literally for the next thirty or so minutes, was a full-scale, eleven-on-eleven football match, played right there, in the middle of the crowd, on the plaza in front of the museum.

Kids ranging in age from ten to fifteen had set up their school backpacks to mark goals on either end of about a quarter of the plaza. The sidelines were unofficial, generally where the senior citizens sat looking on from stone benches, or where the tourists sat ordering *tapas* from bored waiters. But the sidelines were also, in a sense, constantly moving, even sometimes across the middle of the pitch. Those "sidelines" consisted of locals and some oblivious tourists who had absolutely no qualms about walking right through the middle of the game. The tourists may have been clueless to the dangers I initially thought awaited them. But the locals, particularly the senior citizens, tired of the bench of choice, were not. They were familiar enough with these apparently regular matches to know that the space could be shared. They knew that the footballers had sufficient skills to work their way around the human obstacles slowly making their way across the plaza. As impressive as the footballers' ability to play around and through this crowd was the fact that the plaza was sloped, not as a gradual incline, mind you, but as a series of large, twenty-or-so-foot-wide steps gradually descending from the top of the square toward Atocha station.

With so many moving obstacles, we might imagine that this would produce a cautious game, played entirely on the ground, perhaps a bit slower than what you would expect on a traditional pitch. If so, we would be wrong. Instead, the boys played hard, with sharp passes and quick movement. They dribbled with admirable skill, and took powerful shots on goal. The ball didn't just skid along the ground but regularly took flight as players switched fields or countered forward. This was real soccer. For thirty minutes the ball didn't hit anyone but the kids playing. No tourist was injured. The senior citizens went home for the night with nary a scratch. No waiter reprimanded the boys for reckless behavior or demanded they take their game elsewhere. The game happened. And it was beautiful.

So I ask, what kinds of skills would be required to pull off a match like that? What would the consequences be of not having those skills? What would happen if an errant ball was miss-hit into the second row of *tapas*-eating tourists? What would become of their afternoon game?

What skills would such a pitch demand of the kid who wants to be included?

Wanting to Be Included

When Mario was ten years old, living in Trieste in northern Italy he was one of those kids. He wanted to play football, *calcio*. There was a game that he could join, played every afternoon at the local blacktop. There was, alas, one big problem. The pitch was built on the end of a very steep hill. Really more a cliff than a hill, depending on who's doing the looking or telling the story. Two sides safety. Two sides disaster. At least if you miss-hit that ball.

No one needed to explain to ten-year-old Mario that if he wanted to play with the local boys, he'd need to develop some serious ball control, some high-level touch. So Mario, like any normal kid who wants to play ball with his friends, set to work. No coach or parent needed to direct him out back to get his touches. No one needed to steer his attention to YouTube juggling tutorials. No tournament director needed to dangle trophies in his face, to say nothing of coaches threatening benching. The threat of that ball shooting over the fence and over the veritable cliff below, plus the possibility of a long walk in search of the ball, and perhaps permanent exclusion from the game, was more than enough. The only trophy? Being able to play with the big boys.

Mario learned.

What about U.S.?

Let's bring this back home. In 2015, US Soccer announced what some took as a radical revamping of the national youth curriculum. One of the more controversial aspects—at least in some benighted corners of this nation of ours—was the mandate for smaller-sided games through the U12 age group. Fewer players and smaller fields. Even smaller goals! Just imagine.

And imagine some did. The cries of foul could be found on message boards and soccer fields across the United States. The federation was asking the kids to play something that wasn't soccer because, as we all know, the reasoning went, soccer is played with eleven on a side, one of them always a goalkeeper (who, by the way, can use hands), not to mention with an offside rule, plus three referees. The reasoning should have been utterly bewildering to anyone who learned to play basketball through countless one-on-ones and three-on-threes in the driveways of America, or who learned baseball with ghost runners, or played intense games of American football with just two other friends. Still, the horrified reaction could be heard.

Of course such a reaction was not uniform or even the majority. Our own local club, for example, wasn't caught the least bit off guard. Inspired by what we had seen around the world, nearly a decade earlier we had purchased a half-dozen very small goals in order to encourage precisely the very small-sided games US Soccer was finally, officially embracing. We understood that skills development doesn't require a large, spacious, perfectly proportioned field. In fact, it is hampered by such wide open spaces. Perhaps if we'd been really prescient we would have invested in some planters, some sidewalk cafes, or a cliff at the edge of the complex. As it was, we were already taking plenty of grief for those small goals. The goals we had purchased weren't some Pugg-style pop-up things but solid steel structures meant to last at least as long as the full-sizers the club already owned. The expense was significant, and some couldn't see the sense of it.

To this day, certain coaches in the club never use them. They're not "real" soccer goals and the fields they're on are just too small, they apparently think. Several years ago, a coach from another area club spent a year with our program because of some temporary personnel shifts across town.

On more than one occasion, he noted with little attempt to hide the disdain in his voice, that we were the club with the small goals and the small fields. We were the ones interested in "foot skills."

How silly of us. Playing on our small fields with fewer players, each of those players getting dozens, perhaps hundreds more touches per practice, figuring out how to control and move the ball in tighter spaces, dealing with defenders and fellow players constantly invading their space. For shame! Who did we think we were, denying our kids the opportunity to try out their big boot, to hoof the ball as far and furiously down a full-sized field as possible? How cruel to make the kids play on fields that demand, and reward, precision passing and exact shooting. How cruel to engage the kids in tightly packed 4v4s, 3v3s, and 2v2s where they could quickly learn about the angles, the triangles and diamonds around which the offences of all the world's great teams click. If only our ten-year-old left back could spend half of practice charging back-and-forth down that one hundred yard lane waiting with baited breath for the switch of fields that never comes!

Thankfully, US Soccer finally figured out what some already had. Ironically, their curriculum proved a step back for many clubs. Our local travel league actually had to increase the numbers of players on the field to meet US Soccer's new regulations. More players, of course, translates into fewer touches. At this age, as many know, getting those touches is everything. Experts often refer to the years between eight and fourteen as "the golden age" of skills development, when kids are ready to really hone their technique. Indeed it's the one and only time they really can. If you wait until puberty, the legs become too powerful. Kids who haven't developed that soft, caressing touch on the ball just aren't going to be able to after that. Not, at least, if they want the kind of touch to play at the highest levels.

A powerful argument can be made that, in fact, the only games anyone should be playing up until adolescence are the smallest of the small-sided games: 3v3s and 4v4s. They should be playing on fields no larger than half a regulation basketball court with goals matched to size.

If quality touches are the foundation of technical-skills development, which is the foundation of a great soccer player, consider the difference in touches per player on a tight 3v3 field vs the 7v7 field now required by US Soccer for all U9 and U10 teams. In the case of our club fields, that 7v7 field is approximately three times as large as the 3v3 field. Taking into consideration the extra space, the difference in touches is not just the difference between six versus fourteen kids on the field, all vying for time on the ball, but also the difference between the game encouraged by the different-sized fields. The larger the field, the more time that ball spends on its own and not at the foot of the kid who needs those touches. Now calculate those touch differences for an entire season, practice after practice, and game after game. In our typical fall season we're talking fourteen or so weeks of practice (two per week) plus ten games. Do the math. It's going to be a lot of touches.

Now let's add to the fact that a less-informed US youth soccer coach, seeing the larger field and reading the current US Soccer Federation rules, is going to spend her practices coaching the kinds of skills and tactics such field conditions encourage. The touch difference only grows.

Meanwhile, on the Other Side of the World:

Yes, meanwhile, on the other side of the world, in Holland, historically the most successful footballing nation in the world when considering population size against success, or in Argentina, home to Diego Maradona, Lionel Messi, and two World Cup titles, the kids are playing small-sided games.

While it's true that serious players in some of the most serious and successful footballing countries begin playing 11v11 soccer on full-sized fields at around ten years of age. Yet, we should keep in mind that as we've noted in "No Grass," long before and long after those kids take their first 11v11 field, they have honed some serious skills on all sorts of small-sided fields under all sorts of strange, tightly packed, and chaotic conditions.

Johann Cruyff, was one of the greatest players and, arguably, the greatest mind the game has ever known. Through his individual ball mastery and tactical genius, some would claim he single-handedly changed the way the game was played. Cruyff narrates:

> My generation learned to play soccer in the street. Our skill levels greatly improved because of the lack of space, and the fact that there were few of us meant that we were always involved in the game. The street was our soccer school. Players like Pele, Beckenbauer, Platini, Di Stefano and myself all started by kicking a football, tin can, rubber ball or even rags in the street against guys who would fight to get the "ball" off you. You had to rely on your quick thinking and your skill when playing against these guys, because not only were they bigger than you, but there were lots of them and

you were often surrounded. During those games my team-mates were the walls and even the curbs of the pavement. My favorite move was to kick the ball against the wall and control the rebound whilst running at speed as this tenth of a second was often the crucial difference between scoring a goal or not.

Keep in mind as we read this that Cruyff grew up practically in the shadow of one of the Netherlands' most storied clubs, Ajax, where his mother worked as a cleaning lady. Thus Cruyff had early and frequent access to that club's relatively pristine playing grounds. But where was Cruyff perfecting his skills?

Even when Cruyff recalls big games, we discover him playing his most formative soccer in the most unusual of places. "There was also a time when all the schools in Amsterdam took part in a soccer tournament which lasted the whole school year. The games were played in the street and the final took place in the main square. I got the same thrill playing in that tournament as I did playing in the 1974 World Cup." The streets. The curbs. The walls. The town square. The greatest in the world, a boy with access to the training grounds of a professional club. Yet it's the streets he remembers. It's the streets with all their imperfections to which he credits his game.

Where else might tomorrow's geniuses be plying their still-elementary trade? Here are three other possibilities for consideration.

Public School Daoíz y Velarde, Alcalá de Henares, Community of Madrid, Spain

Behold the blacktop before the bell rings to signal the start of another school day. Behold the football matches. While there is only one field—one court, to be precise—one cannot say *the* football match. One must say the football matches. Yes, indeed, on this morning, as on any given morning at Daoíz y Velarde, there is not one but multiple matches with twenty to thirty, maybe even forty kids, with two or three balls, in one small space. They have no choice. The rest of the patio is occupied by kids digging in sandboxes or jumping around hopscotch squares. Close to a hundred parents, grandparents, and babysitters occupy another corner of the patio, visiting, as the very social Spaniards are wont to do, after dropping off their kids. There is, again, no space but one. In that space, multiple games proceed simultaneously. The kids dribble with speed and skill over hard blacktop carefully avoiding not only defenders but the kids chasing the other one or two balls around the same pitch. The pitch, of course, is really just a piece of blacktop without borders but with boundaries that each player implicitly understands and respects. They know Spanish adults aren't as permissive as your typical North American coddler. So don't kick that ball into the chatting parents. Don't run into your sister on the hopscotch court. And by all means, score a goal or two while you're at it.

May the 25th Expressway, City of Buenos Aires, Province of Buenos Aires, Argentina

No, we're not playing on the freeway. We're not that extreme. Instead, for miles a variety of local entrepreneurs and municipal authorities have set up football fields in the dark, loud spaces directly beneath the freeway. Throw up a few lights and a bit of carpet or, if there's money for it, artificial turf, and you've created a place to play. Not large spaces, mind you. The massive concrete structure overhead requires huge support beams, which means frequent blocks of concrete carving up the less-than-ideal footballing spaces. As a result, it's all small-sided games here, no matter the age of the players. Small-sided games with a variety of small-sized goals with sidelines anywhere between three to six inches deep, if that. So is the game hampered? Do players not learn proper soccer? Well, it's Argentina. Last time we checked they'd won a couple of World Cups with an equal number of finals appearances.

Church of the Holy Soccer Field, Corso Vittorio Emanuele, Rome, Italy

No, the game is not in the church. Step instead out of the massive carved wooden doors into the piazza below. The piazza, with marble steps and fountain, is a tight, semicircular wedge crammed between the church's imposing baroque façade and the modern avenue just beyond. There, automobiles, delivery trucks, and emergency vehicles with sirens blaring do battle with the ubiquitous Italian chaos of Vespas darting at breakneck speed in and out of traffic. There, in that ten by twenty meter half-moon of marble and concrete, the kids bring their ball day after day while parishioners come and go. How do they play in such a space? How do they even survive? How would you? How many balls would you lose to traffic before you learned? What would you learn? How fast would you learn it? Again, the football on display is stunning in its speed and skill. Never once does the ball careen out onto the congested avenue just a step or two away. Never once does it strike the façade of the historic church. The game goes on. Is it any wonder the Italians have won four World Cups with appearances in two other title games?

The Elusive (and Destructive) Search for the Perfect Field

Meanwhile back in the USA, we keep looking for more space, for more places to set up perfect soccer fields. We build massive complexes of pristine grassy fields to ensure every team has plenty of room to train in a regulation space. Those massive complexes cost money. We pay those bills, either as taxpayers or as club members, and thus continue to drive what should be the simplest, least expensive game in the world out of the price range of a growing number of families.

Instead of the football played in so many other parts of the world, we create the cultural phenomenon known as US Soccer. A phenomenon consisting of tens, perhaps hundreds, of thousands of upper-middle-class children driven several times a week, often daily, across town, when not the state itself, sometimes for hours at a time so they can train at the perfect soccer space. While their childhoods slowly slip away, they sit buckled and bored in the back of the family SUV with their video games, as mom or dad drives and drives and drives.

Then, when they get there at last, they run out onto a field with so much space and so little challenge that the coach, if she knows and cares enough to do so, must invent game after game, drill after drill, to teach skills that would have taught themselves immediately in the strange shapes and angles, the tight spaces, and the tricky surfaces of the kid's own backyard. There, just beyond her back door she might have gathered with a handful of friends to kick around whatever spherical object they found at hand. Some of those friends might be those potentially very talented kids without the means to make the same trip to the fields of SuperClub FC.

The quest for ideal footballing pitches is not only a colossal waste of time and money for players at the lower ages, but those pitches, once found, arguably do more harm than good. As in the chapter on grass, consider all those dribbling drills rendered unnecessary by simply packing the game into tight, difficult spaces. Think of all those drills and games we imagine or sold to us by enterprising internet coaches who faced the exact same problems a few seasons earlier: fields too perfect, too spacious, and too mundanely uniform to provide the kids with the natural challenges of the game itself. Consider then how much time coaches spend explaining drills and games, purchased or dreamt up. Consider how many of those drills don't even work. Or how many of those players quickly discover that all those pseudo-games are just that and practice is dull and all they want to do is play. "When are we going to scrimmage?" they demand, practice after practice. Anyone who has coached knows the cry.

Consider, in particular those players who are almost exclusively gamers. If you've coached for more than a season or two, you know exactly the one. That kid who gives almost nothing in practice, who shows up late and bored, and who sleepwalks through just about every activity as if soccer were of no interest at all. When you imagine the first game of the season, that player is nowhere in your plans. But then, eventually, at some point in the first half, you reluctantly send the kid to midfield on the referee's next whistle. Then, thirty seconds into what you expect will be a rather uninspired and uninspiring performance, the kid suddenly takes off running like a bat out of hell, fighting for every ball, and scoring those elusive goals that some of your practice warriors can never seem to conjure up come game time. Yes, you've been there. We all have. After the match, we scratch our heads and wonder what that kid would be like if he'd just show up, physically, mentally, and emotionally, to practice. Ah, the lost talent!

But honestly, whose fault is it? The kid wants to play football, the beautiful game. And instead we're giving him soccer drills. Why? Because we've been bred on a culture of overcoaching that, we would argue, is driven in large part by field conditions—thick grass and, here, "perfect" wide-open spaces—that offer no natural challenges.

Shaping Up US Football:

So why don't we simply change the conditions? Why don't we tighten the fields? Why not, instead of three teams spread across three acres, pack six, eight, ten or even more teams into those spaces?

Imagine the crowds. Imagine the buzz of activity. Imagine each of those mini-fields with constant mini-games. Imagine the joy of the kids who, after all, really just want to play the game. Imagine those kids having to maneuver with almost every step around the pressure of immediate defense. Imagine the understanding, quickly developed, that a miss-hit ball is a ball that goes flying off into another game (since we can't just build a cliff). Or imagine the alertness of our players on the already crowded field as balls from adjacent fields frequently enter their own playing space followed by the players from that field coming over to retrieve their ball.

Imagine, as well, the ability of coaches to shift opponents quickly. Is Team A blowing out Team B? Then flip a player or two from one field to the next. Or rotate with teams on adjoining fields. Team A with C, B with D. Occasionally bring in E, F, G, and H, even if they're in other age brackets. Weaker players competing against stronger ones. Stronger players moving up to be humbled by an older group right next door or to discover that they can hold their own. Imagine each kid getting dozens more touches in actual game situations, touches that come naturally without the hectoring of a coach pushing the kid through yet another foot skills drill.

From a distance, what we've just envisioned might look like chaos. But what must a World Cup final feel like? What does it feel like to play before a crowd of 70,000 screaming fans? To have the hopes and dreams of entire nations, the demanding gaze of millions if not billions of aficionados the world over, the withering critique of network pundits and social-media trolls all pressing down on the backs and into the heads of eleven players only several years beyond adolescence? Then add one or two of the very best athletes in the world bearing down on you at breakneck pace, bound and determined to dispossess you of the ball and if necessary destroy your limb if not your life in the process. How does that feel?

Football *is* pressure. Football is, when played with intensity and passion, chaotic. Football is the unexpected, the impossible angle, the fake and the feint, the imaginative, innovative, genius, split-second understanding of surprise spaces opening up for micro-moments that spell the difference between the thrill of victory and the agony of defeat. Is that the game we're introducing to our children on US soccer fields around the country? Is it any wonder then that our kids are ultimately unprepared? Is it any wonder that out of a base of millions of little tykes running about chasing a ball, we've never, not once, in the history of US Soccer been able to produce more than a half dozen or so players competing at any given moment in Europe's top leagues (being generous with that designation).

Our problem, again, is a grassroots one. We're doing things wrong at the youngest ages. We're making conditions too perfect, too clean, and too spacious. But this is nothing a simple return to chaos wouldn't solve, a simple reduction of space, a simple change of shape. The rest will follow. And when the soccer moms and dads cry out, "But this isn't soccer!" we can answer with a smile, "Of course not, it's football." Welcome to the world's game.

7. No Travel

Several weeks into a course I was teaching at the local university, I at last had the chance to talk to the student on the back row, the one always wearing the latest gear of a major university in an adjoining state. After a bit of small talk I asked, "What's with all the University X gear?"

"Oh, I played soccer there last year."

As a soccer enthusiast and a fan of our own college team, I was intrigued. "So, did you finish up your eligibility and transfer back home?"

"No," she cheerily answered, "I just decided I was tired of it all."

She went on to explain that she had played continuously since age three. Essentially her entire life. By age five or six, she clearly had talent. So her parents moved her from the local program to an outstanding girls club in the area. There she spent the next twelve years, playing so much soccer, travelling so much, and missing so much school that it appeared she wouldn't graduate.

In the end, though, it all worked out and paid off. She won a scholarship to a nationally ranked program at an outstanding public university. Even better, once there, despite being a true freshman, she stepped right into the starting lineup and played every game at attacking midfielder. She was living the dream, athletically and academically.

Except that the dream wasn't hers. In fact, almost as soon as she arrived at her new school, she realized that, deep down, she lacked true passion for the sport. She had achieved her goal—or perhaps her parents' goal—of a Division-I scholarship. What was left to accomplish? Without desire, why continue? And so, after completing the season and finishing her fall semester, she dropped out and returned home to attend the local university.

Our conversation continued. Surely, I figured, she would be lacing up her boots in a less high-pressure situation for our own university team. They were going through a rough spot and could use her.

"No," she said. "I room with the girls from the team. They're my friends from club days. But for now, I'm happy to be a student."

As a soccer parent myself, I paused to take in what she had just told me.

Then, mustering up my courage, I threw out the final question: "And your parents?"

"Yeah." She smiled, for the first time, a hint of guilt creeping across her face, "They're not very happy." Then she dropped the real parent killer: "Especially because my sister has decided to stop playing as well. She's a striker, four inches taller than me and super fast. She was being recruited by North Carolina. But when I quit, she realized she actually felt the same way. So she's done as well."

And with that go the dreams of... not the two girls, because, of course, it wasn't their dream. They merely happened to have talent ("Sure, we enjoyed hanging out with our friends, winning, getting lots of attention," she told me). The dreams were the parents'.

It was a conveyer belt that she and her sister—both blessed with a healthy dose of talent and a willingness to put in the work—jumped on to be carried along whether or not they cared deeply about the game they were playing. It had been enough that her parents, coaches, and the system itself cared. It worked. But not for the two sisters, or in other words, for the players, or, worse yet, the *children*.

Travel Soccer
In the United States of America, most children begin playing soccer sometime between ages three and six. Their journey begins when their parents sign them up for some kind of local program that requires little more than a drive

to a nearby park. The program charges fees that cover simple field use and processing. Coaches are typically parent volunteers. It's low-key stuff. Just kick a ball around after you've learned how to walk. Anyone can do it. Most everyone does. It's lots of fun, for kids, parents, and neighbors.

Then, sometime between age six and nine enters the great divide. That's when all the little tykes who've been scoring all the goals and dominating the ball—looking, in comparison to their less gifted peers, like little Messi's and Maradona's—get scooped up into more competitive leagues, leaving behind, typically forever, their pals from the playground. They make the move, per the parents, in order to play with other equally talented kids. Time for another challenge. The next level.

These select kids are clearly better, and so, to continue improving, they clearly need both stiffer competition and higher quality coaching. So the process begins, first as the kids and their parents travel from park to park in search of equally elite teams, then from city to city, and eventually, if all goes well, from state to state if not country to country. With every level, the competition ramps up as does the quality of the coaching. With a bit of luck and hard work, the young player will continue to improve and develop in their quest to fulfill the Messi-like potential first flashed at the local park.

And that is how you become a soccer star in the USA. That is how you develop the skills that catapult you into football's biggest leagues. That is how you develop the talents that lead the US every four years to the World Cup and increasingly close to that elusive final. That's how US soccer grows. That's how stars are born.

Except of course, none of that actually happens.

World Cups? Big stars in the biggest leagues? How about mere second-tier stars in second-tier leagues

(Cue sound of crickets).

Still struggling?

(More crickets, please).

Yes, so are we.

Bummer.

The sad fact is that in 2018, forty-plus years after the youth soccer explosion of the 1970s and with now millions upon millions of kids playing and travelling in the system described above, the USA couldn't field eleven players capable of beating or even tying what experts described as the second-string team of Trinidad and Tobago.

We are the richest nation in the world, yet we couldn't win against an island nation of 1.36 million people (that's Dallas, Texas, folks) with a per capita income of $31,870, to qualify for the biggest tournament in sports, the ultimate dream of every kid who every laced up a pair of boots. But it wasn't only Trinidad and Tobago. We were only in that fix because we couldn't beat the likes of Panama, Honduras, or Costa Rica. These are countries with populations of 4.3 million (that's the city of Los Angeles plus Long Beach), 9.11 million (that's the state of Michigan), and 4.86 million (somewhere between Louisiana and South Carolina) respectively, with per capita incomes of $23,000, $5,300, and $16,400. We, in comparison, boast a population (read talent pool) of well over 325 million, with a GDP of $18.558 trillion and per capita income of $57,400. In terms of human and monetary resources there is no comparison. Yet, as far as regular starters in the world's major football leagues—not stars, just starters!—we boast anywhere from one to three, depending on how you count them.

So what's going on? In other chapters of this book we explore the on-the-field approaches at the clubs where US soccer goes to die.

But what about the clubs themselves and the leagues in which they play?

What about the conveyer belt my student jumped on, the system of coaches and coordinators and parents that moved her along for more than a decade before she could catch her breath and realize she didn't actually care?

What's going on in US youth soccer?

Perhaps the simplest way to begin is via a bald statement that football is a game; soccer is a business. We acknowledge that this idea has its limits. Still it's a place to start, one that should provoke some thinking, something we should all be engaged in a bit more as we stare at the state of our footballing world.

While true that football these days is big business in almost every corner of the globe, historically in other countries that has not been the case with the youth game. There, football is indeed business at the top. In contrast, here in the USA until very recently the only money to be made on the sport was at the bottom. Unlike in the world's football-mad countries, where multiple levels of professional clubs created resources for a lucrative market for the buying and selling of rights to players, the lack of professional clubs in the US plus the relative lack of quality of US players meant no financial rewards for developing American talent. There was little money to be made in football at the top of the US Soccer pyramid.

But there *was* money, and plenty of it, in soccer in the suburbs where the young professional parents of the 1970s and 1980s sought a safe, more urbane alternative to American football and basketball.

Organized soccer served first as day care and then later as an ego massage to stressed-out yuppies living vicariously through children who had become as emotionally priceless as they were economically worthless.[1]

Every self-respecting entrepreneur with a bit more soccer knowledge than the upwardly mobile parents and (ideally) a hint of a British accent recognized immediately that they were sitting on a cash cow. So they opened a dairy. Actually, lots of them.

So today, thousands of people with varying degrees of soccer knowledge and a nose for money have created a system in which parents pay for their mini-Maradona's to play what is sold as ever-higher-level soccer. If your kid shows promise in the early years, you can almost guarantee that the travel clubs will come a-calling, selling to you what they will market as superior coaching and resources. The praise is flattering, and to the average US parent, relatively ignorant of things football, the siren song proves irresistible. Upper-middle-class helicopter parents do not require much convincing to invest in their children.

Better coaching? You bet.

Fancier uniforms? Why not?

Lengthier travel, even overnight stays for weekend-long tournaments? Just another sign that this is serious.

Travel soccer in the US has become very big business indeed. Thousands of coaches across the country earn themselves comfortable livings from clubs designed to recruit and retain as many players as possible in order to fill out as many rosters as possible—or at least as many as necessary to keep the wolf from the door if not the BMW in the garage. Now, how do you most easily recruit and retain when many of these well-meaning and well-moneyed soccer parents have little soccer background, and in many cases no clue? Well, you look the part.

Meaning, you win.

And you lie.

Harsh? Perhaps. But before we dismiss such a cynical notion, let's explore a bit more.

Let's first take on the question of lying. If it makes us feel any better, let's call it in more genteel fashion mere truth-stretching. Let's even acknowledge that it is sometimes innocent and perhaps rarely intentionally cynical.

But let's explore. If you've got a club to form and teams to organize, you need players. How do you get those players? You say what needs to be said, and you learn as fast as you can to believe that you're telling the truth. (Trust us, we've been there.)

So you approach parents and spread the word that kids need better coaching and better teammates and a more competitive atmosphere at increasingly early ages if they ever want to fulfill their potential—whether or not you have any supporting evidence. Once that truth becomes universally acknowledged among the parents on all those local parks and rec soccer fields, you set out in search of the local stars—which it behooves you to define rather broadly. Next, you find the parents of the kids who stand out. You tell them that their kid in particular has potential and they should seriously consider allowing him to take the game to the next level, and so on and so forth. After all, the kid shows something—maybe a spark of passion or a bit of vision or some soft feet.

And did we mention that the coach needs players?

He needs that team of second graders in order to keep the club going, the fields paid for, the assistant coaches under contract, and the people believing he runs a serious operation. Ultimately his mortgage has to be paid. So he says whatever needs to be said to get as many people to sign on his dotted line. He hones in on a sliver of a kid's talent, often revealing only a piece of the whole picture, both his and the kid's. So he creates teams of seven-year-olds that most likely didn't need to be formed in the first place.

The pattern, sadly, though predictably, continues all the way up the ladder, multiplied by thousands, even tens of thousands, maybe hundreds of thousands, across the nation. And so the dishonesty continues year after year, because whether or not someone belongs, their money belongs, and that is the bottom line. The consequences are far reaching.

But let's move on to the part about winning before we double back.

Pay-to-play programs need to win. To convince people you're worth money, you must promise to deliver quality. Again, since few of us are trained to see quality, we are easily fooled by victories (not to mention easily upset by losses).

Now, if you've got to win, how do you coach? You coach to win, of course. Any coach with any experience can tell you that the way to coach winning soccer is not always compatible with developing talent. In the youngest age groups size, speed, and strength almost always carry the day, especially on the thick grassy fields where Americans typically play.

So put out the big kids, let them hoof the ball up the field and then send the fast ones to chase it. Oh, and keep the biggest, most athletic kid in goal. Don't let the other team score, and you win. Play safe, defensive soccer. Kick the ball out of bounds any time danger strikes. Also, tell your players what to do. Be explicit about it. Don't let them make too many mistakes. Play them in the same positions game after game so they know exactly what to do, and don't forget to give them very specific instructions about those positions. Finally, occasionally berate them when they make mistakes. In practice, devote significant time to working on set plays and tactics. A young team that knows how to score off corners and free kicks against a bunch of boys naively honing their technical skills is going to win almost every time. Do that and the wins will come.

At least at the younger ages.

But in the meantime, what's happening with the kids? Who is learning to dribble? Who is learning to make her own decisions? Who is learning to think about the game from every angle of the field? And what about the poor kid stuck in goal, game after game after game?

All the Children Left Behind

In the meantime, while your child has been (dishonestly and cynically) yanked into the travel ranks, there was probably still plenty of progress to be made in her recreation league, where something very different is happening with the kids abandoned back on those old parks and rec fields.

When they show up the next year for the first game, the fields are emptier and the quality has declined. They play, but perhaps with less energy and enthusiasm.

The sifting process then begins anew, this time at an even more accelerated rate. In the absence of the mini-Maradonas from last season, the okay kids begin to feel too good for the less-than-okay riffraff. They too decide to jet. Next year's rosters will be even thinner.

Within a few years, the local low-cost program will probably fold at the upper-age levels. In larger markets, perhaps enough kids will still be around to keep things going. But the people in charge will likely pay them little heed, allowing them to run around the field almost totally unsupervised, without any qualified, quality coaching. They're the leftovers. Sadly, there may still be a few kids with real potential running about in that mix. These are the late bloomers whose continued love of the game might have fostered a more soccer-friendly climate in the local community if they had been given a chance to develop. They might have eventually challenged the mini-Maradonas long since departed into the more prestigious travel leagues.

While kids are jettisoned, more destructive still is the message this process sends to the community as a whole: the simple but devastating statement that soccer is not their game. It's not the community's game. It's not, in the end, America's game. It's a game for toddlers and elementary school kids. It's the first game kids play but also the first they abandon. Those kids may recall with fondness and a bit of self-mockery their passion for pink shin guards and Power Ranger soccer balls. But now it's time for the "real American sports" football, basketball, and baseball. The kind the people play.

They'll maintain some awareness that soccer continues to exist somewhere out there, a game being played by wealthy suburbanites. Most Americans, however, will have never actually seen any of the games this exclusive group engages in. We only see the players as their parents pack them into their SUVs and cart them off every afternoon to some elite, far-away sports complex where they engage in high-level training programs that spit them out after the sun has long gone down and the rest of us have settled in for the night. We see them leave for weekends at a time, driving to other exclusive sports complexes in other far-off suburban communities. We see them pull up late Sunday evening, sporting large plastic trophies and a back seat full of fast-food refuse, evidence that something must have happened, that somewhere soccer exists. Without the little tykes, the local soccer fields would be dormant. The local parks feature kids shooting hoops or riding skateboards, hanging out on the swings. But there is no soccer. Anywhere. The people are doing something else.

Baby, I'm Worth It

But surely, while we're sacrificing the grassroots, there must be a lot of great competition taking place at these specialized complexes where the most precocious talents of each town meet to do battle?

Unfortunately, not in our experience.

In order to understand this, it is helpful to see American soccer, like our flat earth, as turtles all the way down. The first turtle is the local recreation league. The next is likely a localish travel organization. From there we move on to the regional super clubs, which in turn are trumped by a handful of super-super clubs that will dominate state or multi-state play. At each level, the club at the next level up cannibalizes the ones at the level below and so on until we arrive, again, at the now thoroughly gutted neighborhood recreational leagues. It's a long, tragic process of poaching and watering down through more false promises of precocious talent and more damaging displays of "winning" soccer.

To understand a little better, let's take a brief look at our Midwestern region of the country where three super clubs compete for the best male players from a couple dozen or so local clubs. While these super-clubs field their own teams of six-and seven-year-olds, every year new players from the surrounding local travel clubs are enticed to move up to the supers. So each year the local travel leagues become weaker and weaker, while the super clubs become richer and richer. By middle school many of the local travel clubs can no longer field teams. Once again, very talented kids without next-level financial means are left behind, their talents wasted as local programs fold, or they find themselves playing against new travel teams cobbled together from the remnants of the now defunct local parks and rec programs.

Now it's not only the grassroots but the next level up that is suffering. Again, the message to the kids left behind is, as it is to the kids in the parks and rec league, that soccer is ultimately a sport only for the elite. The only difference now is that this time those elite are the super-elite, that is, either the very, very best players or the very wealthiest, or some combination of both. So, even at the level of travel soccer, real talent continues to be wasted and a potential rising tide of quality players disappears to be replaced by the message that soccer is still not the people's sport.

But surely the move must be worthwhile for the kids who do actually make it to the super clubs? Aren't they at least able to play with ever better teammates, being coached by ever more qualified coaches, against ever keener competition?

Again, not necessarily.

In my son's most recent U14 fall season, his team—part of one of the three super clubs in the area—played ten league games and three weekend tournaments. Eight of their league games resulted in lopsided victories, one upset loss, and one other somewhat close affair. Luckily, they told us, we had the tournaments. These, they promised, would offer more elite competition. Yet, out of three tournaments, the kids still faced only one truly challenging team.

How is this possible? With all the best kids moving up to these super clubs and the super clubs playing each other, shouldn't the challenge and the quality increase proportionally?

Perhaps, if there were any quality control. But again, let's look locally at the same three super clubs. While the three recruit from the same pool of local talent, each club at the U14 level plays in a different league. One plays in the local state league. Another travels to the state to the north, while the third travels even farther to the east to play in two other adjoining states. Having observed the kids in these three clubs up close over the years, you'd think they could save a lot of time and money by playing each other a couple of times each season, while adding a handful of games against other super-club teams in nearby urban areas. Why would they each sign up for different leagues and regularly drive, sometimes up to ten hours for a single game—not to mention the tournament travel—when there is solid competition in their own backyard?

Apparently, there's a sales job going on here that requires quite a bit of smoke and mirrors. To play the local competition might reveal too much. To travel—the further, the better—however, creates myriad excuses and subterfuges. Look how far we go in search of the best! Look who we play! And look how much we win!

But when you're playing teams no one's ever seen up close, how can your average, relatively soccer-ignorant suburban parent judge what they're seeing on the field? They see wins. For most, that's enough. The rest is hazy, but they wouldn't know. What *is* fairly clear, to those who know to ask the right questions, is that each club tries really hard to keep the parents happy and the players enrolled. Whether or not the kids are challenged at the proper level is an afterthought.

So, is there value in moving to a super club? In the case of my own son, he is clearly playing with teammates superior to those at our local club. We finally chose the super club because our own local club's Director of Coaching recommended a greater challenge. But two years in, we're not convinced that the lopsided victories he's enjoying with his teammates provide that challenge. Perhaps he would have been better off faced with the responsibility of being a leader on his former team? What about the impact on the kids in his former club if he *and others* had stayed? Wouldn't they all be a little better? What about all the friendships my son left behind? What about all the driving? If he did have to leave, why isn't he playing against all the other kids from the region who also left their local teams? Why are they all in separate leagues? Why are all three winning the majority of their games while our region continues to underperform in sending kids on to Division-I college programs, to say nothing of professional contracts? Something seems to be amiss here.

High Stakes, Poor Play?

Sadly, we haven't even touched yet on arguably the most fundamental problem with the competitive soccer system in this country, the problem eating at the root of the tree and preventing the US from developing the creative talent to win World Cups.

Let's begin, as we often do, with a question: what kind of a game can only be played when in an official uniform, on an official field, after paying official money, under the constant and frequently withering gaze of anxious adults? In other words, how does a game work when that game looks less like a game and more like work? What kind of a game is a game that can be played only under constant pressure after countless hours of drills and chalk talks? What kind of play results when the play can't even start until just the right jersey and shorts and socks and underwear and caps have been donned, when shin guards have been recovered from the back seat of the SUV, when mom is finished stressing because the shin guard was lost and dad is done steaming because we're gonna be late? What kind of a game requires officials—whom my team's coach, parents, and players and even the other team apparently despise (except when the calls go in our favor)? What kind of skills develop when any mistake committed incurs the wrath of sideline parents or the frustrated cries of a coach and leads to a loss of playing time? How does any of that inspire creativity, experimentation, and the simple joy of free play?

Now, if so many questions give us too much to think on, it's okay. That's because we'll have plenty of time to consider it all as we drive increasingly long distances to practices and games in our never-ending search for better coaching and better fields and better competition, with mini-Maradona sitting in the back with a Gameboy or iPhone while the years pass by as we drive and drive and drive.

How many hours of our lives, we wonder? How many hours in a youth soccer lifetime? How many hours for that student of mine who decided after a year of college that she really wasn't especially passionate about soccer? Well, let's pause for a little simple math.

Here are some modest estimates based on one parent's experience at a mid-tier travel club in our area for the hours driving for one year of soccer (fall and spring outdoor season plus winter indoor season).

• Practice: fall and spring seasons: 1 hour drive round trip/practice x 4 practices/week x 12 weeks/season x 2 seasons = 96 hours

• Practice: winter season: 1 hour round trip x 2 practices/week x 8 weeks = 16 hours

• Home games: 5 games x 1 hour round trip x 2 seasons = 10 hours

• Away games: 5 games x 4 hour round trip x 2 seasons = 40 hours

• Tournaments: 3 tournaments/season x 2 seasons x 6 hour round trip = 36 hours

Total: 198 hours driving/year

Let's do the math. If your kid plays travel soccer from second through eighth grade, you're looking at well over one thousand hours of your kid's being stuck in the back seat of a car while you drive her to places to "play." Sounds like fun. In the case of my student, beginning in her middle school years, those tournaments became increasingly far flung. First, all over the Midwest, then eventually out to the coasts. How many hours did she and her family put in? The calculations point in the direction of Malcolm Galdwell's famous 10,000 hours of practice required to become expert at anything![2] Unfortunately for your kid, that's 10,000 hours in the back seat of a car, not 10,000 hours honing the craft.

That should give us pause.

We'll let you and yours consider the effects on your wallet of all that driving, all those hotels, all those annual player fees, plus the annually updated uniforms, and the fuel and repairs on the car that drives and drives and drives.

Need we mention how little scholarship money is actually out there for the average graduate of these travel clubs, let alone how unlikely it is that any of these kids will ever enter the professional ranks? The money matters are on you. Suffice it to say, that's a lot of cash. Now keep in mind that all that effort, all that stress, all that money, and all that time will likely result in little but a closet full of outgrown uniforms and a shelf full of plastic trophies. Have you ever considered why these trophies are plastic and not gold, silver, or bronze? Maybe because they really are not worth anything. Now if you're into collecting plastic trophies, fine. But all that plastic is not likely to ever be anything greater than just what they are: plastic trophies. Personally, we can think of better ways to spend our hard-earned cash and better ways for a kid to spend her childhood.

With the above in mind, let us summarize with a somewhat long-winded but terribly important question. How many World Cups do we think we're going to win with a system that: (1) deceives itself and others by recruiting and retaining players with dishonest player assessments that favor money over talent; (2) rewards coaches who win rather than coaches who develop players; (3) continually waters down local programs, leagues, and clubs, essentially destroying local soccer for anyone beyond early childhood and preventing almost any possibility for soccer to become America's game; (4) turns soccer into a business and youth players into mini pro athletes (with the irony that the mini pros are the ones who are paying to play) where the game is about long, tedious travel, expensive uniforms, and high-stakes games and tournaments?

The answer is sobering.

But what can we do? Well, to begin, we can do the opposite. That is, topflight player development at the organizational level must first, be honest and fair to kids and parents, encouraging development if and only if right for the player as a whole person. Second, player development must focus on developing the player—not on winning, making money, or any other matter that might distract from that goal. Third, it must sustain, grow, and improve soccer at the grassroots level, ensuring it be seen by all as the people's game, the game of all Americans, and not just as some elitist suburban whim. Fourth, it must allow kids to be kids with conditions that encourage them to play the game as a game, to spend their 10,000 hours playing with joy and freedom instead of driving and driving and driving only to perform for coaches and parents in search of bright plastic cups, ribbons, and medals.

Are these four recommendations even possible in the current system? No, at least not as long as club owners and operators make money by convincing people to join their clubs with displays of winning percentages, participation in prestigious far-flung tournaments, or lengthy travel for the superior competition their brand supposedly deserves.

But if this is the system, how do we fix it?

Reimagining Football

As those familiar with soccer in this country know, there are solutions from the top that would begin with transforming the MLS, USL, so that they mirror the rest of the world. There clubs operate their own academies where they develop youth players. Profits come by showcasing those players on the pitch and then either promoting those players to their professional team or selling their contract rights to other professional clubs. If money can be made via player purchases at the top of the footballing food chain, then the lower end shifts from winning to development. When money is made by selling the rights to homegrown talent, the focus of clubs becomes the development of truly special players, whatever their income levels. These players will be vital to the interests of the next level of clubs, which, in turn, will be very careful about developing *their* investment. The pressure on clubs and coaches shifts immediately from wins and losses to making the most of each player in the system. Money comes when the player has been developed, not when his team has won yet another tournament.

When player development becomes the cash cow, the rest of youth soccer becomes, well, just games. In other words, the kids will likely find themselves playing more, with less pressure, without worrying about having "enough" substitutes, without worrying about having players who can play the "right" positions, and without worrying about getting every last call on the field right. We'll have a game that will again become a game, something that will likely be more fun, not only for the players but also for the coaches, the parents, and even casual fans, who might just begin showing up to watch for entertainment, as they do today with American football or basketball.

Games focused on player development would be more joyful, more holistic. Coaches, fans, parents, and players would start seeing a bigger picture on the field and would begin celebrating not just the goals scored or prevented that produce a result but great plays, visionary passes, brilliant runs, control under pressure, and solid defending. One can imagine the effects of such a change of focus, not only at the top but all the way to the lowest levels. How much more pleasant might the whole experience be for nearly everyone? How much more might such a sport grow? How many more excellent players might the sport retain? How much more easily might such a sport become America's game?

But such questions are still all pie in the sky if we can't imagine a system where clubs buy out the contracts of players all the way down. How would that look?

Before offering some thoughts on the topic, let us be clear that we understand the complexity of reorganizing soccer at the professional level. Still, it's worth at least thinking through the most basic elements of a transformation. In the US, a reorganization would begin with MLS clubs doing one of any combination of three things. One, they would purchase player contracts from USL and other professional clubs. Two, they would develop them in their own academies. Three, they would purchase them directly from super-regional clubs. At the next level down, USL and other lower-tier professional operations would purchase their player contracts from the super-regionals or, of course, develop talent in their own academies as, again, is done in the rest of the footballing world. Through this model, professional clubs (MLS, USL, etc.) pay super-regional clubs for their best players. Those regionals in turn pay super-city clubs for their best players, who in turn pay local clubs for their best players. Four layers down should easily get you to the grassroots of American soccer. Or perhaps there should be only three levels. The fewer levels, the better. Because the real key is precisely the grassroots where the vast majority of kids do not need to travel. After all, for the vast majority of players soccer will probably never be anything more than a game.

But that doesn't mean players not destined for high-level play should be neglected. The real key to developing our handful of outstanding talents is to keep as many hard-working, passionate-playing, fun-loving kids as close to home as possible. There, at their local playground, they would play as many small-sided, low-key games as possible, day after day after day. Instead of 10,000 hours driving, we'd have kids enjoying thousands more hours playing, not to mention thousands more dollars lining our pocketbooks. A rising tide of soccer players could lift everyone's boat.

Play to Play

How about a step back to consider why we're doing any of what we're presently doing in the first place. Unless you have an actual financial stake in a travel club, the answer is you would never invent a system like the one we currently have. Football is first and foremost a game played by kids. Whether or not our kid is the next Messi, we want him to fulfill his potential by playing, as a player and as a human being. If our kid *is* the next Messi, we want to be sure that he or she can be properly and honestly identified for development at a time as objectively appropriate as can be had. In the meantime, we want him to grow up in an environment where the best possible soccer is being played by the maximum number of kids. But potential will only be fulfilled where the game thrives and competition abounds. Competition and encouragement from peers, more than anything else, will keep passion for the sport alive and will push him to excel during the early years, when technical-skill development peaks. What we certainly don't want is for our kid to spend half his childhood in the back seat of planes, trains, and automobiles, isolated from friends, doing the will of a cadre of anxious adults who discover all too late that the child was just riding on a conveyor belt.

We want the beautiful game for the next generation of millions of children who want to play. Ironically and importantly, simple, beautiful play will lead to mini-Maradonas and World Cups. Anything else is more of the same. We've already seen where that has taken us.

8. No Bench

After the fall season, a U10 squad preparing for a winter 3v3 indoor tournament had six players sign up. The question was whether to field one team or two. Considering the objective of entering the tournament was for the kids to play, the decision was made to field two thinner squads. Sitting on a bench on the sidelines is not playing. One of the teams performed well enough to reach the championship game. The other did not, but was satisfied because they had been able to play.

The opposing team in the final made the opposite decision, entering one squad with seven players continuously substituted in and out like a hockey team. The fresh energy of the newly entered players allowed them to press and run at a rapid clip, a beehive of activity. The coach of the 3v3 team somewhat naïvely asked if his two 3-player squads could combine for the final. After all, they were all members of the same U10 team, and they all wanted to play.

The officials approached the coach of the seven-player squad to ask if there were any objections. The retort was that such a change would be unfair and did not abide by the terms of registration in the tournament. Technically that was correct.

The same coach had arrived at the tournament that morning in a V-8 muscle car; an engineering marvel able to vroom over one hundred miles per hour in a few seconds. Such capacity was perhaps useful on the German *autobahn*, where there are no speed limits, but was overkill on American roads with a speed limit of seventy miles per hour.

Is there an analogy here?

In the championship 3v3 final our three-player squad faced the seven-player squad. The game was tied 1-1 at the half. In the second half, the seven-player squad, aided by fresh substitutions, rampaged to a 6-1 victory, and their players took home a plastic trophy. In hindsight, the coach of the three-player team should have understood the mentality of American sports and offered to forfeit the piece of plastic. The two teams could have played a 6v7 friendly game. Yes, one team would have had one more player, but so what if the other team had an extra player? In this manner, the seven-player squad would still get their plastic trophies, but the final would have been more competitive and allowed participation of more kids. However, even this approach would have been flawed. For the game and the reaction of the coach of the seven-player squad revealed a fundamental aspect of American sports culture with regard to substitutions.

Substitution versus Individualism

American football, basketball, baseball, and lacrosse allow unlimited player substitutions. Participation in these "American" sports means not only playing the game, but being constantly on the lookout for antics from coaches who can substitute at will, affording an advantage for teams with extra players. Like the coach of the seven-player squad and his cool muscle car (don't get us wrong, we think muscle cars really are cool), the rationale for having excess capacity, or horsepower, is for it to be there if needed. So the driver, or in this case the coach, can win based upon management of resources.

But children are children, not resources. The point of play is for children to play. Not to sit on a bench. Soccer is the most popular sport in the world because it is cheap, a poor man's game, a player's game rather than a coach's game. All one needs is a ball, and even that can be made out of a sock and some rags as we saw in the "No Balls" chapter.

Substitution in American football is so invasive that teams are divided into three separate squads: offense, defense, and the special teams assigned to kickoffs and transfer of possession. Gone are the leather-helmet days of greats like Sammy Baugh who played quarterback, punter, and linebacker for the 1940s Washington Redskins. Basketball coaches have been known to field two separate teams in a single game. In his heyday as basketball coach at North Carolina, Dean Smith fielded two, five-member squads for wholesale substitution at his discretion. Baseball has complex rules about substitutions for designated hitters, pitchers, and field players - surprising for a sport where players spend at least half the game resting in the dugout.

In contrast, soccer with its maximum of three substitutions at the professional level, could be considered the last "player's game." In soccer's original rules, "substitution" referred to replacing players who did not show up for the game, not to players replaced at a coach's discretion for tactical purposes. Substitutions were not even allowed in the World Cup until the 1970 tournament. The limit of three substitutions has added tactical nuance to the game. In its DNA blueprint, soccer limits substitutions with initial rules allowing a number under conditions agreed upon by contesting teams and the referee before the game.

Rule Fiddling

Attempts to fiddle with the rules of a game are a comprehensible impulse. The rules for soccer originated in England but transformed into something loved by the entire planet, not just the sons of British imperials prancing about the muddy fields of Eaton.

Offside once required three players (two plus the goalie) to be behind an offensive player making a pass. This was later reduced to two players behind the pass (one player plus goalie). Now passes back to the goalie must be done with the feet to speed up the game. Upon its inauguration in the early 1990s, the MLS tried to reintroduce the tiebreak "shootout" because ties were considered un-American. Baseball goes to extra innings to avoid them. Basketball and American football extend to overtime periods. Rule changes happen and sometimes they stick. So change is not impossible nor should it be proscribed.

Changes in substitution rules, however, simply turn soccer into a different game. In the college game, NCAA rules allow unlimited substitutions in the first half. Players substituted in the first half are prohibited from return until the second half, when again there are unlimited substitutions with a substituted player only allowed one reentry. High school soccer has no limits on substitution at all.

Unlimited substitutions are another facet of the less-is-more dilemma facing US soccer. The culture of unlimited substitutions hinders the technical development of individual players by rewarding the advantages of the physicality achievable with constant waves of fresh, fast legs platooning into the game at every break. A game without substitutions rewards the technical ability of the individual or the mental ability of the team to adapt. Substitutions do the opposite. Indeed, as their name indicates, they substitute, reducing and even eliminating advantages gained from head-to-head competition. A stream of fresh players can press and charge with a short-term intensity that devalues technical ability, and may promote injury.

So how do unlimited substitutions teach kids creativity, thinking for themselves, or solving a problem on their own? They don't.

Tactical or strategic problems become the territory of the coach rather than the players. Unlimited substitutions cause the American game, particularly in the high school and college games, to suffer from overcoaching. The power of the coach to control who enters the game and for how long through unlimited substitutions reduces the freedom of the players to interpret the game according to their wits. One of the key lessons of sport is how to overcome adversity, but such a lesson should not only be physical, but also mental, about strategy and tactics. Brawn is good. Brawn plus brains is better.

The limitless substitutions currently allowed in the high school and college game in the United States have handicapped development of a sector which might have provided an advantage. Most other soccer-playing nations lack vibrant and well-funded high school and college leagues. The US Soccer Federation's attempt to reform youth soccer in 2007 with the US Development Academy system devalued high school and even college soccer to the point of advising the prohibition of academy players from playing high school soccer.

The result has been a decline in the numbers of men's national team players who played high school or even college soccer. Bruce Arena's men's national team, which arrived at the quarterfinals of the 2002 World Cup, had players from the University of Virginia and DC United, reminiscent of how many national teams rely on a nucleus of players from the most successful domestic professional club.

Rather than devaluing an entire section of the American game, the soccer player in high school and college, for replacement with the US Development Academy in 2007, a long-term approach would have sought to correct the deficiencies in the scholastic divisions. Well-developed high school and college sports leagues have vast infrastructure, rich traditions, and ready-made fan base. These advantages are unique to the US. So why not allow the high school and college systems to develop? With the simple tweak of changing substitution rules to comply with international FIFA regulations, the high school and college games could become an asset. No need to reinvent the wheel. Just take advantage of what America already has to offer.

Cool Whip

This impulse to replace and substitute rather than to fix may be explained in cultural terms as the "American replacement of nature."[1] The common analogy is that all one needs to make cream is a cow and some elbow grease. In contrast, manufacturing a can of compressed creamlike substitute like *Cool Whip* requires an entire commercial and industrial apparatus.[2] The *Cool Whip* culture, not the cow, put a man on the moon. But soccer is not rocket science. The game could not be simpler. Unless one has an allergy, real cow cream is healthier than an artificial cream substitute with preservatives and chemical additives. Artificial concoctions may be more pleasing to the eye but are of questionable value to the physical well-being of the consumer. Why be enslaved to bells and whistles when all we are talking about is some kids kicking a ball?

This replacement of nature carries over to American sports, and particularly to American football, where the human participant has been transformed into a muscled specimen pumped up by anabolic steroids. The human's natural protective coating, skin, is replaced by a hard plastic helmet with plastic-covered metal bars and plastic pads. Recent NFL rules allow certain players intercom receivers in their helmets to be nagged by the coach in the middle of the game, replacing the player's brain with that of a host of experts on the sideline and even in the press box.

The natural course of time is still an unfettered part of baseball. American football and basketball are controlled by a clock, which can be stopped for timeouts, change of possession, and other excuses, like TV commercials. Timeouts are particularly counterintuitive. Allowing one team to stop play prevents the team that was winning from exploiting advantages to victory. American football even stops play for something called the "two minute warning," which to people unfamiliar with the game seems comical, as if both teams were not smart enough to figure out that the game is about to end.

Substitution and the replacement of nature may be useful in some instances, like going to the moon, or finding a nondairy creamer to help with your lactose intolerance. In a game as simple as soccer, however, they are distractions that prevent player development.

9. No Coaches

The Klinsmann Verdict

Jürgen Klinsmann, the former US men's team national coach, leveled a devastating verdict on US soccer. In Spanish, the term to describe the national team coach is neither "coach" nor "trainer" but *seleccionador*, which may be literally translated as "selector" or "chooser." The role of a national team coach is not so much to teach the best players in the country as to choose the right mix for a successful team.

Klinsmann's scouting and recruiting efforts as "chooser" focused on professional youth academies abroad. He wanted players who had grown up abroad but could attain US citizenship, as if the best chance for the US men's national team to qualify for the World Cup was to have a team as uncontaminated by homegrown American players as possible.

The soccer backgrounds of the best US players confirm Klinsmann's prejudice. A disproportionate number of players on the US men's national teams had parents who were either former players, coaches, or somehow affiliated with the game. The winner of the 2016 Hermann trophy for the best college soccer player went to Ian Harkes, son of former University of Virginia standout, John Harkes. Other players for whom soccer was the family business include members of the disgraced 2018 men's national team: Demarcus Beasley, Michael Bradley, and Christian Pulisic. The latest American young hope is Timothy Weah, son of George Weah of Paris Saint Germain and Milan fame in European football.

Such players should provide added value to a nation's soccer elite, but cannot be its only resource. In a sustainable system, the raw material for a nation's soccer elite should come from the general population. Anyone who has ever compared a perfectly symmetrical hydroponic tomato to the rough but tasty produce from a home garden understands the difference. Produce created under perfect, artificial conditions is indeed quite spectacular. But the raw flavor of a natural product is what makes a meal or a recipe.

A Good Coach Thrives with Good Players

Bruce Arena is the most successful American soccer coach of all time. He won championships at the University of Virginia, DC United, the LA Galaxy and managed a stunning run in the 2002 World Cup, eliminated by Germany in a tournament marred by officiating that was, to be diplomatic, "regrettable."

In 2017, Arena was on the sidelines as his US men's national team lost 2-1 to Trinidad Tobago on Black Wednesday, a result that eliminated the US from the 2018 World Cup. Arena had fielded a team of players mostly from the MLS in the critical return leg, where the US needed only a tie to qualify. His approach was opposite of Klinsmann's preference for players trained and playing professionally abroad. Arena endured criticism for this strategy, even being accused of "patriotism." In the long-term, his decision revealed the US system's weaknesses. Failure may not be much fun, but it can be a good teacher.

Arena's coaching persona is seemingly gruff. However, often successful coaches limit themselves to providing technical and moral support with decisions that earn the team's respect. Even a compliment from a coach may be misinterpreted as a veiled criticism by evoking past failures or inviting comparison to the faults or merits of teammates.[1] In this vein, Arena's coaching acumen allowed players' physical reality to direct their efforts without inciting the active, waking mind, the ego, due to distraction from second-guessing a coach's decisions. Arena's pragmatic approach has deep roots in American culture and offers a tradition to be valued.

Arena's cool demeanor in the embarrassing circumstances of the postgame press conference after the Trinidad and Tobago catastrophe was typical of his ability to retain a sense of decorum. With typical aplomb, Arena urged the nation that all was not lost. The course upon which the USSF had taken the American game could use some adjustments but should not be abandoned.

However, Arena's optimism was incongruous with such a defeat and contrary to our premise that indeed everything *is* lost. Everything will continue to be lost without a transformation in American soccer from reliance on grass fields and equipment to a culture based on the essentials of street ball that can produce the quality players an able coach like Arena requires for success.

A Virginia Soccer Coaching Experiment

In his early days as a college coach at the University of Virginia, Arena's recruiting focus was in the soccer hotbeds in the northeast, his home turf. Despite this, in the summer of 1980, he sought out local soccer talent. Local high school players from central Virginia were invited to a free clinic, what would now be called a combine, organized by with Arena's assistants and attended by other college coaches in the region. The first day consisted of technical assessments and one-on-one drills, which degraded into scrimmages. The next day, the absence of Arena and his staff was noted by all. Evidently there was not enough raw material in the area to warrant further attention.

Before the start of the spring high school season, one of Arena's assistant coaches contacted a pair of those high school players. He invited them to Virginia's Memorial Gymnasium for 6:00 a.m., five-day-a-week sessions in what amounted to a soccer experiment. The idea was to see if the level of the kids could be brought up to the standards required in college play.

One of the kids had played street ball abroad before settling in the US as the child of immigrants. The other had moved from the state of Washington, which had an established soccer scene even in the 1970s. Both could play at a basic level, but neither had exceptional skills nor physical attributes. In the soccer culture of the day, the two high schoolers played only during the spring season.

After assessment with cone dribbles and the like, the focus of every session became juggling. The two high schoolers and the assistant coach would juggle the ball in the air to one another, first one touch, then two touches up to ten touches, after which they would descend down to one touch. The two high schoolers had never seen much football juggling before. There was no internet in 1980. After several weeks, the high school players mastered the game and developed an approximation of touch common to competitive youth players around the world. The two high school kids went on to a successful high school season and opportunities to play in college. Still, the exercises at this Virginia soccer experiment were remedial by world standards. Children destined for academy soccer in the world possess such skills by the time they are ten-years-old or much younger.

The exercises that the Virginia coach proposed would never have occurred to the two kids on their own. This is the true role for youth coaches: to identify weaknesses and to implement exercises and activities that allow children to raise their skill level, with demonstrations to overcome technical deficiencies, whether an inability to juggle, overdependence on one foot, or whatever the technical lacunae. However, to be most effective, a coach must have players with basic abilities and with a basic, cultural understanding of the game.

Arena saw that the best high school players in central Virginia in 1980 were so technically deficient that only a pair were worth the effort of development. The experiment conducted by his assistant confirmed the assessment. High-level coaching can be effective only if there is the raw material and ability on hand to benefit from instruction. Bruce Arena shone as a coach when his players were good enough to compete, as his record from the University of Virginia to DC United and in the 2002 World Cup attests. During the US qualifying run for the 2018 World Cup, this was not the case. Arena could not perform the miracle of making a diamond out of the rough of the players on the 2018 men's national team.

In the US, grassroots player ability remains at a remedial level, which reduces the possibility for elite-player development. The solution has been to camouflage that deficiency with the window dressing of equipment, training, travel, and organized coaching. Elimination from the 2018 World Cup revealed that the emperor has no clothes. What American children need is to practice and then play and then practice and play some more and then play even more so that coaches have the raw material at hand to prepare players to compete at higher levels.

America's Player Gap

One would think that, since 1980, the level of play and technical skill among America's youth would have significantly improved, and to some extent, they have. Bruce Arena's successors scouring central Virginia for talent would find kids playing at a higher level than in the early 1980s. Yet, in terms of skill at an international level, the US continues to lag far behind.

Proof that the current system has failed lies not just in the embarrassment of elimination from the 2018 World Cup but in the unflattering values assessed to players from the current US Development Academy system on the international market. The US suffers in comparison not only to the world's leading producer of players, Brazil, but even to Iceland, a nation with a population of less than

350,000. Players developed in the US system recognized as having professional potential are advised to go to Mexico or to Europe to hone their craft. The lack of marketable homegrown players and the lack of profits from contract buyouts have hampered the US Development Academy's mission to serve as a conduit for the American professional league, the MLS. At best, the US Development Academy has developed a generation of NCAA Division-I college players and some MLS-level professionals, but not world-class professionals.

Ben Speas, from outside Cleveland, Ohio, was the best player from the Crew Junior Academy in the past generation. He scored the winning goal in the NCAA Soccer Cup in 2011 and received a local player contract from the Crew. However, his career languished thereafter with release to the MLS Minnesota United FC, and then to the Indy Eleven of the now defunct NASL, the equivalent of second-division soccer in the United States.

The lack of homegrown players is not for want of heroic initiatives. In 2005, former US men's national team goalie and later U19 and New England Revolution coach, Brad Friedel, quixotically funded an academy in his hometown of Loraine, Ohio, outside Cleveland. Friedel's Premier Soccer Academy had a business model based on the idea of offering training to US talent and then recouping revenue from contract buyouts. Unfortunately, the players recruited and trained in Friedel's academy did not attain sufficient contract value to maintain the facility, let alone turn a profit. The real pool of potential players from which an academy like Friedel's could draw should be huge, the entire 300-plus million population of the United States. But unfortunately, the pool was much smaller, limited to those few groomed to attain a certain level of technical proficiency. Friedel's elegant institution was sold at sheriff's auction in 2011.

American Coaching Culture: "Winning Isn't Everything, It's the Only Thing."

Bruce Arena's approach to coaching could contrast with American football coaches including Ohio State's Woody Hayes, whose win-or-die attitude led teams to inevitable defeat against the more relaxed West Coast squads of USC and UCLA in Rose Bowls of the 1970s. Hayes embarrassingly ended his career by punching a player on the Clemson Tiger football team in the middle of a game. Hayes came out of the coaching style espoused by American football coaching legend, Vince Lombardi with his dictum, "Winning isn't everything, it's the only thing." Can anyone imagine Bruce Arena punching an opposing player in the middle of a game?

Basketball has more of an affinity with the beautiful game and was reportedly invented by James Naismith so that his charges, who had been playing soccer outdoors, could get some exercise in the winter. Basketball originated as a game where a soccer ball is bounced and shot into baskets with the hands rather than the feet. Of course, basketball also has its Lombardi-like characters such as Bobby Knight, the former Indiana University basketball coach, notorious for throwing furniture and annoying his players.

The irony of this high-pressure coaching ideology is that its proponents are not the most successful. In basketball, coaches like John Wooden, Dean Smith, and Phil Jackson espoused a Zen-like cool in their demeanor and were much more successful than Bobby Knight. Of course, it is easy to remain calm as a coach with players like Michael Jordan and Lew Alcindor, who could make any coach look like a genius.

"No Pain, No Gain."

Urban Meyer arrived at Bowling Green State University as head American football coach in 2001. After

123

the first week of practice, one third of the team reportedly threatened to quit, overwhelmed by the physical duress of Meyer's regimen, which included 5:00 a.m. workouts.

Such an approach may be effective in American football where physicality is more of a requisite than skill, but it does not translate to soccer, where the slowest player on the field may be the best, like Andrea Pirlo, man of the match in the 2006 World Cup final.

The presumptions behind Meyer's coaching methods emphasizing physicality, or the take-no-prisoners gruel *alla* Hayes from American football in particular are not entirely applicable to soccer, where skill and wits may trump physicality and even tactics. In soccer, an intelligently passed ball can travel faster than any human can run. Pressing is most effective against a team with technical weaknesses. If a team is technically proficient enough to rarely give away the ball, then pressing and relying on physicality has limits. As noted earlier, FC Barcelona coach Pep Guardiola quipped that in his vision of a perfect game the opposing team would never touch the ball.

There Is No "I" in "Team"

In formative years, the selfishness of a young child to hog the ball and to try new moves is a positive attribute. Technical skill in soccer is best honed before puberty. A child who does not undergo a selfish stage may lack the technical skill for higher-level play when the role of team tactics and strategy may be introduced. This reality of soccer development runs contrary to the "no 'I' in team" mantra of American team sports.

US soccer coaching certification addressed the issue of individualism versus team play with the stated goal in coaching courses of promoting individual play rather than tactical awareness until age twelve. In USSF licensing courses, candidates learn that until age twelve, children should not kick the ball out of bounds on defense in order for the team to regroup. Instead, a child should try to play out of a difficult situation to develop skills and value individual ability over result. A kid who gains confidence with the ball will have an asset that will yield higher, longer-term returns than winning a little league game.

The motivation of these initiatives is noble and well intentioned. However, it runs contrary to American coaching culture and earns the disdain of parents and coaches with backgrounds in the "no 'I' in team" mentality. There are anecdotes of children in America who learned to play in the freedom of street-style football but were upbraided by coaches fearing individual initiative as an obstacle to team cohesion. Even worse, coaches at all levels of American soccer and even worldwide may unfortunately give in to the temptation to tap into their inner Woody Hayes and instruct their charges to foul and upset a talented player on the opposing team as a route to victory.

Americans have tried to impose the culture of teamwork over individuality to the extreme of providing "participation" trophies or medals. The idea is to instill the communal values of team play according to the "no 'I' in team" mantra. But rewards for all devalue experience. A trophy has value if it is rare and results from achievement meriting recognition.

The conflict between coaches focused on team virtues versus individual player brilliance remains controversial in soccer even at the highest levels. Roberto Baggio, golden boot in 1994, had coaches, including those at the national-team level, who were reticent to include him in their squads. Any strategy proposed by the coach was inevitably rendered moot once Baggio's teammates realized the best tactic was simply to get him the ball near the goal. A similar condition hampered the Argentinian national team in the 2000s when Lionel Messi's teammates threw most tactical ideas out the window for one play, "Get Messi the ball." The resulting lack of team chemistry almost cost

Argentina qualification to the 2018 World Cup, only attained when Messi heroically scored a hat trick in the final qualifying game. Clearly, having a national team dependent on an exceptional player can be a pitfall. However, after embarrassment of elimination from the 2018 World Cup, an abundance of individually exceptional players would be a welcome change for US soccer.

America's Coaching Gap

The deficiency in the current US coaching system is not a lack of enthusiasm on the part of the instructors. Instead, problems are a consequence of their soccer culture. Most US coaches have playing experience at the US high school, college, or in the odd instance, MLS level. None are world-class in terms of technical ability, tactics, or style of play. Many coaches lack the spontaneous, natural ability with the ball that is born of the streets. If that basic cultural connection is not established among the majority of American children, then the efforts of even the best coaches will have limits.

US soccer can also be like a closed fraternity, even locally, where people who played together since youth leagues in a region tend to favor their comrades and neighbors rather than outsiders. Another issue is the expense to attain a high-level coaching license, which can run into the thousands of dollars, and which are often available only after travelling vast distances to the select places where coaching license courses may be held. Attaining a USSF C, B, or the highest-level A license requires course fees, travel, lodging, plus time away from work and family.

If You Can't Beat Them, Hire Them.

Silvio Berlusconi bought the Milan football club when it was languishing in the Italian serie B second division. As club president, he led the team to a string of serie A and

Champions League titles. He did not do so by developing local talent, an approach which has negatively impacted Italian soccer. Since failing to qualify for the 2018 World Cup, Italian soccer may be in a state of crisis even graver than that facing the US. Yet, Berlusconi did have one strategy that could be applicable to US coaching. When Berlusconi's team faced an opponent with a top player, Berlusconi would simply buy the player. Instead of playing against Milan, Marco Van Basten, Ruud Guulit, Andrei Shevchenko, George Weah, and Clarence Seedorf donned the Milan *rossonero* uniform and led them to championships. If you can't beat them, hire them.

When a system has failed, as the US soccer youth system has failed, a rational reaction is to evaluate successful competitors to see what may be learned, copied, and hired. Americans have already succeeded in nonindigenous sports such as gymnastics by hiring outside expertise to raise the level of American endeavor. The US Soccer Club Association has courageously imported coaching expertise from Spain's La Liga, sponsoring seminars and clinics for the nation's club soccer coaches. The USSF has instituted online courses for grassroots-level licensure of coaches, who then may enter into the professional D to A license track. These are valid initiatives. However, a more effective strategy may be to determine who has the world's best-structured educational system and simply do what they're doing. So, where are the world's best soccer coaches?

An Icelandic-coaching Moon Shot

Contrary to common belief, the greatest soccer nation in the world is not among the victors of the most recent World Cups. As of the writing of this chapter, arguably the greatest soccer-playing nation in the world per capita is the frigid, volcanic island nation of Iceland with a population of a little over 300,000—about the same as Corpus Christi,

Texas. If Corpus Christi, Texas had somehow seceded from the Union, qualified for the 2014 World Cup, and made the quarterfinals after defeating England—now that would have been a story. For some reason, the US soccer establishment has not taken note. Iceland, unlike the US, Italy, and the Netherlands, qualified for the 2018 World Cup and did so in the highly competitive European group stages. Iceland's very qualification for the World Cup is a huge victory and point of pride for such a small nation.

Iceland has natural disadvantages that one would think would prevent it from becoming a mini soccer power. An Arctic climate, short summers, and rocky volcanic terrain mean that grass fields are unavailable much of the year. Icelanders play in covered field houses on artificial turf. This apparent handicap is actually an advantage, since Icelandic footballers are unhampered by the *pratomania* grass-field obsession, afflicting US soccer.

Secondly, the country's small population has been turned into an advantage. With so few potential youngsters physically able to participate in sport, the notion of eliminating players through successive weeding and testing, is impractical.[2] In Iceland, *all* players develop to their maximum potential under a massive cadre of highly competent coaches. The country boasts the highest number of UEFA B license holders per capita in the world.

The Icelandic people recently experienced a political revolution resulting from the financial and political failures of their establishment elite.[3] From 2008-2011, the country's financial system suffered a collapse that left much of the previous establishment elite in disgrace. The nation experimented with direct democracy and limited government spending, which allowed the country to thrive both economically and culturally. This political revival extended to the country's soccer establishment, tired of being a doormat in European international competition. The Icelandic Soccer Federation focused on raising the technical ability of young players with the most rigorous and universal coaching certification and licensure program in the history of the sport, which produced in turn all those UEFA B license holders.

Why not take a page out of the Berlusconi strategy and hire the people who created Iceland's soccer curriculum? After certification by UEFA in Switzerland, why not put the Icelandic soccer curriculum online for free? The obstacles of cost, the buddy system, and the problem of distance may be solved through free online courses for licensing to the UEFA B level.

Course instruction should follow the old-school educational method of having candidates transcribe material longhand, followed by audio self-recordings of that same source material, written summaries, and finally commentary in their own written and spoken words. Competent graders could examine the submitted longhand and audio material for correction and re-correction by the candidates until error free. The entire portfolio should be graded on a pass/fail basis. Either the candidate transcribed, recorded, summarized, and commented on all the material competently, or they did not. Licensure must guarantee capacity at all levels, whether professional or grassroots, particularly since the source of any vibrant national soccer culture is the grassroots. What if airline pilot certification required only knowing eighty percent of the material? Would that mean that they could do everything except land the plane?

The current USSF emphasis on face-to-face, live interaction between educational staff and students is anachronistic in the current online educational milieu. Online education can facilitate access to resources. However, this should not decay into dependence on the easy access of digital information as a replacement for memory and proficiency.

Previous designations in the USSF accreditation system differentiated between levels D to A, later expanded to F to A. We were suspicious that these additional levels of licensure were a way to increase the number of products and hence profits. There was also a differentiation between state and national licenses, as if it were permissible to be less qualified within one's state of residence than in every other state. In 2018, the USSF eliminated the F and E licenses and established two tracks: one professional and the other grassroots. Perhaps this change was in reaction to the looming US soccer crisis following the revelation of the twenty-five percent drop in participation.

If questions of cost, distance, and the buddy system may be resolved through online education, then the question of quality and content is more complicated and will face entrenched interests within the current system, about which we have no illusions. For discussion of the question of whose interests should be paramount, the system's or the citizen's, please see the "No Complex" chapter ahead. A free, online Icelandic-model curriculum could produce the best-educated and largest cadre of qualified coaches in the world. These proficient coaches could share their knowledge from the humblest recreation leagues to clubs, high school, college, semiprofessional, and professional levels—a coaching licensure moonshot!

What American soccer does not need is a foundation upon coaching ideologies that find their best application in American football. Instead, the US could benefit from a massive dissemination of world-class soccer culture. This could be attained through an inexpensive or free online education modeled on a successful example like that from Iceland. With tens of thousands of potential youth coaches—not to mention soccer parents themselves—receiving higher-level training, we could provide the more soccer-appropriate coaching that our children need at the most basic, grassroots level of American soccer. As we take care of the kids at the earliest ages who should be US soccer's bread-and-butter, we'll raise a generation and then a second and third who will begin to play en masse the game at a level comparable to the rest of the world. Then able and pragmaticcoaches like Bruce Arena will have what current American soccer culture does not provide, great players.

10. No Parents

If we could magically send a letter to our younger selves twenty years ago—a "Dear Younger Selves"—this book might not exist. We admit having made most (ok all) of the errors described below. Moreover, we realize that even with the benefit of advice, we might likely repeat many of our mistakes. Parenting is perhaps the hardest job there is. Which is why we should probably all just stay as far away at times as we can. For now, for what it´s worth, here´s the letter we would have written to ourselves, so Dear Younger Selves:

Potty Training

What does potty training have to do with being a soccer parent? Before the late 1960s, most large American cities still had diaper services, which collected soiled diapers and provided paying parents with clean, cotton diapers weekly. With the arrival of disposable diapers, parents could just toss the soiled disposable in the trash, clean the child's posterior with a chemically laced, disposable wipe, and put on a perfumed, unsoiled diaper as if the "accident" never occurred.

Parents in the same countries without extra money for soccer balls or shoes also do not have extra money for disposable diapers. Rarely will a child above age two in such places need to be potty trained. In contrast, in developed countries, potty training and reliance on diapers can reach into the fourth and even fifth year of a child's life. This plays into the hands of disposable-diaper manufacturers, who make every effort to ensure comfort in the diaper and retain a customer as long as possible.

Is the entire apparatus of the American soccer culture like a huge diaper that inhibits the problem solving and creativity that is at the heart of the beautiful game? In potty training and in learning to play soccer, less may be more. The natural instinct of a parent is to provide more. But if less can be more, more just may be less.

Baby Parking

Sometime around the late 1970s American parents began to fear letting their children play outside unsupervised to roam neighborhoods with friends and unleashed dogs. Soccer rose to popularity because it seemed to offer a solution for American parents desperate to counter a culture where children risk obesity because of sedentary pastimes like video gaming. The old Latin saying *mens sana in corpore sano* (a healthy mind in a healthy body) is a goal shared by parents across cultures and class.

American parents were attracted to organized soccer as a solution. They were drawn by the democratic aspect of the sport's physical requirements. If a child is not tall enough for basketball or burley enough for American football, then parents often opt for soccer. The minimum expectation is for the child to get some exercise in a parent-approved environment on a soft, grass field in shin guards. The maximum expectation is to learn something of value, to gain expertise in a pastime that they will cherish for the rest of their lives and maybe play in high school or even college. Instead of just "baby parking" sanctuaries, parents need to consider why their children should play soccer in the first place. What of value does the game teach?

Having "Fun"

There is a saying that the way one plays soccer is the way one plays life. If a child relies on talent but lazily does not come back on defense, then that is a character flaw that may be identified and corrected through soccer. If a child is an excellent team player, always reliable and stalwart, but does not have the inner confidence to develop individual talent, then that is a character flaw that may be identified and corrected through soccer. Once upon a time, children learned such lessons in the rough-and-tumble culture of the playground by observing older children and measuring their abilities and skills against their peers. Unfortunately, in the United States and the West, the culture of neighborhood pickup games has waned. We propose the creation of an American soccer culture not dependent upon equipment or even coaching, but upon interaction with peers in a setting that will satisfy nervous parents. The goal is for children to become good at something, which is the true definition of "fun."

US parks and rec departments and even clubs have recognized the sterility of the club, drill, and coaching approaches to teaching soccer and have tried to defend their cash cow of paying parents. They are wary of the existential doubt, "Did you have fun?" The origin of the word "fun" from Old English is, "to make a fool, to be a fool, or to cheat and hoax." The notion of "fun," begs the corollary philosophical question, "Are we having fun yet?" where something supposed to be fun is anything but "fun."

Playing ugly soccer in front of screaming parents and obsessed coaches with dreary schedules of travel to practices and tournaments is expensive, time consuming, and stressful, but not "fun." The goal of playing soccer is not to get a plastic trophy or to giggle at a participation medal, but to be good at something, to be able to take pride in efforts that lead to a satisfying result. Building on character strengths while developing physical stamina and strength are valuable capabilities soccer can impart.

Here the news for US soccer is good. The level of play in the US has increased because children and parents are more and more familiar with the game, both as players and as spectators. Many parks and rec departments and clubs have instituted optional pickup practices, where children of different ages may enjoy playing together without lectures or standing in line for drills so they can have "fun." This is an instance where a structure has been put into place that can create a soccer culture.

Soccer Moms and Pops

The recent decline in youth soccer participation may have occurred because American parents are beginning to understand instinctively that there is something amiss with how soccer is taught and played by children in the US. The frustration is palpable on the sidelines, where parents anxiously endure the spectacle of the bunching, long-ball affair that characterizes much of American soccer. The yelling and even screaming from parents, whether at the referee or at their own children, has become so unseemly and even frightening that many clubs around the country have instituted strict behavior guidelines, requiring parents and children to sign legally binding code-of-conduct statements.

Parents spend money on club fees, uniforms, and travel to tournaments. Then they see that recently arrived immigrant children (from those countries clever enough to get their kids out of diapers early) are likely to be better players than their own children upon whom so much time, money, and effort has been spent. Concentrating on the basics, what is ultimately some kids kicking a ball, could prevent some of these tensions.

Parent Coaching

Neither the interests of the parent or the child are typically served by having or being a parent-coach (trust us, we've been there). A child learning to play soccer in a parks and rec league will likely be taught by a parent coach who grew up playing baseball, basketball, and American football, rather than soccer. Unfortunately, the generous parent-volunteers who form the backbone of parks and rec soccer in the US sometimes lack a cultural background in the game.

The other pitfall of parent-coaching is that children approaching puberty seem like they are genetically conditioned to block out the parent's voice, as if there are only a certain number of times, especially in the teenage years, that a child can really listen to a parent. Perhaps those admonitions and words of advice should be spent on matters that will determine the child's future, like studying, choosing the right friends and activities, and getting a job.

Delusions of Grandeur

A sign at one field encouraging parents to behave at games reads, "We are sorry that you did not become a professional soccer player, but that is something that yelling at the referee, the coach, or your kid will not change."

In the soccer-scouting world, the decision on whether a child will enter a professional path comes by age twelve and even earlier. In most soccer-playing nations, chosen children enter elite training academies which are like boarding schools run by the state or professional teams. These children attend soccer practices during the day and have tutors for basic education.

The chances of arriving at the top are slim. The physiological changes that may occur over adolescence can transform a prodigy into an also-ran. Professional sports careers are also short and may end abruptly after injury.

Germany's vaunted scouting and youth training system has been credited with success in reversing the fortunes of the national team from a humiliating elimination in the group stages of the 2000 European Cup to World Cup champion in 2014.[1]Although, Germany's recent national team success has coincided with an influx of immigration, which may have increased the technical level of street ball in the country. Despite the rigorous nature of the German system, the percentage of graduates who actually become professionals is quite small. Even in established soccer-playing nations like Germany, perhaps children would be better served by pursuing training in activities more relevant for their future livelihoods. Perhaps for most, soccer would be best left on the playgrounds rather than the training grounds. Parents whose children shine in parks and rec leagues are tempted to continue into the club pay-to-play system with the hope that their child may play in college or even become a professional. However, the return on the time and money is rarely, if ever, worth the investment.

The Soccer Social Club

This book presumes that American children are blessed with stable home environments, solid nuclear families, and disposable income. With the understanding that this is not always the case, let the recipe herein to base US youth soccer on a recreation of street ball serve as an inspiration for after-school soccer-based activities that tap into the resources of the nation's educational system. There could be after-school programs offered to single- and dual-income families that make use of vacant gyms and black tops at most schools in the country.

Some of the social functions that were once the territory of places of worship or civic associations have been replaced by the trip to a practice, game, or tourney. Here parents meet the other parents and may even make some friends. This seems benign enough, but if the prime mover for these interactions has fundamental flaws, as is the case with US soccer, then perhaps effort may be expended to correct those deficiencies, so that the activity and its social benefits are in everyone's interests. Recalling the anecdote from the "No Travel" chapter of a college athlete who quit the sport once she had some autonomy, parents must be sure that the routine and logistics of club soccer do not take precedence over the interests of the child.

"I Am the Walrus"

One of the weirdest Beatles songs begins with the lyrics, "I am you and you are me and we are all together" followed by a psychedelic stream-of-conscious run through nursery-rhyme fragments and Lewis Carrol references. In the song, John Lennon was not singing about life as a soccer parent. But if the current American youth soccer system had a theme song for parents, we could do worse than choose "I Am the Walrus."

Parents cannot help but live vicariously through their children because they recall periods of their youth as they see their child mature. Yet, this can have a darker side if the parent is living by proxy, with the child fulfilling the unlived experience of the parent. A quick look at a list of psychological terms offers the idea of "enmeshment," where boundaries between people can blur.

The issue for most, ourselves included, is simpler. It is about being needed and realizing that as the child matures that all-consuming parent-child connection will wane, as it should. All the travel to practices, games, tournaments, acquiring proper equipment, and caring for inevitable injuries allow parents to remain as central figures in their children's lives. The travel soccer and club system allow this to persist as the child matures into adolescence and early adulthood. At college soccer games, there is often a group of parent supporters accompanying the away team under the excuse that they are fans. The more likely explanation is that they hope to retain that parent-child connection that gave meaning to their lives when both they and the child really needed each other. In the Lewis Carrol poem that inspired John Lennon, the Walrus character was not a good-guy. To quote another British popstar, "If You Love Somebody, Set Them Free."

11. No Positions

My first year coaching a U8 boys' team, some parents wanted to know why their child, who had scored lots of goals in the parks and rec league, was not scoring goals in club play. Even worse, their kids were taking turns playing defense. "Yuk!"

Parents all over the world, not just Americans, are culturally conditioned to want their kids to play forward. That is the position they demand: not midfield, not defense, not goalie, but forward. Parents want their kids to score goals, and to score goals, the parent surmises, their child must play forward.

So, how to decide who would play forward? I introduced juggling competitions at the start of practice. The number of juggles is a number. Numbers can be measured. The more juggles, the better. Whoever could juggle the most would start at forward. Then the kids could switch positions over the course of games, to learn each position. I could just as easily have set speed as the criteria for playing forward with a footrace at the end of practice to determine the position. But American kids are deficient in ball skills, so juggling it was. This only created more angst for parents who feared their child's exclusion from the "starting forward" club. There were tales of tearful children juggling under the vigilant eyes of their parents and the warning, "If you don't juggle at least ten times, the evil coach will not start you at forward!"

In hindsight, that was probably not all bad, except the stress of parental coercion as fodder for psychological counseling once the kids became adults. At least the kids were practicing at home instead of eating chips, guzzling sugar drinks, and playing video games. What I could not do was change the cultural outlook that valued scoring and playing a certain position, forward, over every other factor in learning the game.

Are Strikers Necessary?

The position of striker in soccer can be a bit of a mystery. The highest scorer in the history of the World Cup until recently was not Pele, nor Maradona, but Gerd Müller, a striker on the West German teams of the 1970s. Müller did not look like a rock-star, goal-scoring machine. Kids in the day did not hang up Gerd Müller posters in their rooms. Yet, when Müller was anywhere near goal, he found a way to put the ball in the back of the net. His goals were not flashy exhibitions of technical or athletic prowess, but of timing, cunning, and an intangible ability to be in the right place at the right time.

Coaches often choose the fastest, the strongest, or the most technically gifted player as forward. In accordance with the unpredictable essence that makes soccer the beautiful game, the player who should play forward is the one who puts the ball in the opposing team's goal most often. However, that player may or may not be the strongest, fastest, or most technically proficient. Like the rest of the game, scoring can be unpredictable.

Some famous teams did not even field a striker. The Spanish team that won the 2010 World Cup created a stir by occasionally not playing any strikers at all. The Spaniards applied the notion of the *false nine*, the traditional jersey number assigned to the center forward, who was, at times, on the Spanish championship team, just another midfielder. Why isn't my kid playing striker? Ask the 2010 World Cup champions.

The team with the best strikers does not necessarily win the game. Having too many strikers who consider themselves too special to come back on defense leaves a team lopsided, spread out over the field, and vulnerable to counterattack.

The 2004 European Championship game was between a workmanlike Greek team, considered lucky to the reach the final, versus Portugal, led by world-class, offensive superstars. Portugal vaunted a young Cristiano Ronaldo. Luis Figo was a recent *balon d'or,* player of the year, award winner. There was also the talented, intelligent, and versatile midfielder, Rui Costa. Some of the Portuguese defenders were stalwarts on top clubs in the English Premier League and Italian serie A top divisions. The salary of the entire Greek team could be covered several times over by the yearly earnings of any of these Portuguese superstars. Portugal was playing at home, supported by an adoring and wildly enthusiastic crowd that thrilled at their heroes' attacking style. On paper the game looked to be a rout.

In the championship final, the Greeks bunkered around their goal as the Portuguese squandered chance after chance. Then in the second half, the Greeks made a humble attempt at a counterattack and earned a corner kick—their only one of the game. The ball was headed into the back of the net by Theodoros Zagorakis, the Greek captain who played on the Italian team Bologna the year of their relegation to the Italian second division. After the Greeks scored, they gained confidence, while the Portuguese superstars became nervous, finding themselves incapable of evening the score.

Having the best forwards does not guarantee victory. The beautiful game is not always fair and can be unpredictable, one of the reasons it is so beloved. Journalists jokingly compared the Greek victory to having Claudia Schiffer, the top supermodel of the period, lose a beauty pageant to a cleaning lady. Apart from the prejudicial presumption that cleaning ladies are not beautiful, the comparison has an element of truth. A supermodel would probably not be willing (or able) to do what would not bother a cleaning lady in the least—like play defense.

How many of the players on that Greek team were playing forward? Nominally, there were a couple. But since the Portuguese had overwhelming technical superiority, the Greek forwards were trying to close passing lanes and get a body in front of the attacking player with the ball just like their defender teammates.

If the circumstances of a game require players to be able to shift in and out of positions, and to have the skill set to do so seamlessly, then why is there an emphasis on playing any position, including forward, at younger ages? The Dutch football style of Total Football meant that a football player must be "total," must be able and comfortable to fill any role on the field. In soccer, playing a position should be secondary to being able to play.

"Play Your Position!"

This brings us to the question of a "position" as geography rather than mental or technical skill. One of my first experiences in youth soccer was as parent co-coach with a former NCAA Division-I basketball player, now a computer-science professor at the local university, for a parks and rec team of six-year-olds. The games were 5v5 plus goalies, which created a mathematical conundrum of how to organize substitutions for the ten children on the team to be divided by six positions, for two twenty-minute halves.

The co-coach arrived at the field in a baseball cap, pen in hand, clipboard ready with a detailed, statistically coherent plan that allowed each child an exact and equitable amount of time in each position. Two twenty-minute halves with ten players would comprise four hundred player-minutes, which divided among six field players, meant 66.6 player-minutes for each position, which divided among the ten players came to 6.6 position-minutes per kid.

The math seemed fuzzy to me, but I was not the computer scientist. So I smiled and proposed that I would not interfere and would be happy to run the next week's game under the same terms of non-interference.

In the first weekly game, the team ran according to a substitution and position-switching regimen, which required yelling at the six-year-olds about being in the right position and switching at 6.5-minute intervals, duly noted on a clipboard. What the kids learned from the system was not so much how to play soccer as how to obey orders.

The next week, I divided the players into two groups of five. Each group played one entire twenty-minute half. Any benched kid who wanted to play goalie was welcome to volunteer to do so. The kids not playing in the official game went to an adjacent field to play 2v2. During the game, I sat on the bench and watched the kids play. No yelling.

The computer scientist/basketball player was not upset but had clearly experienced a culture clash. The benefit for the children of playing the entire the game was understandable, even if they were not on the official playing field. The point of contention was about positions. In basketball a sense of position is paramount.

The six-year-olds in both games had bunched up around the ball like pigeons fighting for breadcrumbs. In most of the world, children have seen enough soccer on television or at recess to understand that the ball travels faster than anyone can run. When one team bunches up around the ball, that leaves open spaces for exploitation and fast breaks. This was not the case with the American kids, who bunched up like bananas.

The solution of the former NCAA Division-I basketball player/computer scientist was to emphasize the maintenance of positions. Each child had to accept

143

responsibility for a section of real estate on the field. The child could even ignore what was happening on other parts of the field, which were the responsibility of other kids. A child assigned to play offense was discouraged from running back on defense. Conversely, children assigned to play defense were prohibited from crossing midfield. To keep this team shape among a team of six-year-olds who had not played or seen much soccer required a great deal of encouragement (also known as yelling).

In a game with twenty-two players on a full-size field, orthodoxy about maintaining positions makes a certain amount of sense. A single player cannot run quickly and consistently enough to cover the entire field for an entire game, particularly if there are no substitutions. When there are fewer than eleven players on the field, as in the case of a 5v5 game of six-year-olds on a reduced-size field, then the idea that any one player should consider herself only a defender or only an attacker is irrational. The result was that some of our six year-olds spent the game standing in a prescribed area like baseball outfielders. They had to be encouraged (yelled at) to stop looking for four-leaf clovers and get into the game when the ball came their way. What did those six year-olds take from the experience? They came to play, but had ended up as the objects of an exasperated parent volunteer. Playing should be fun. Being yelled at is not. Video games anyone?

In street soccer around the world, one notices the fluidity with which players shift in and out of positions according to the circumstances of play. This approach developed into the Dutch Total Football style where players enjoy some freedom to interpret positions according to circumstances. The Spanish *tiki-taka* style further evolved this concept by the elimination of the forward as a set position.

In American sports, playing one's position is the paramount guide to interpreting what to do on the field.

However in soccer, and particularly in small-sided youth games, this is not the case. Learning to maintain a position, no matter the circumstances, like a soldier under orders to defend a hill in battle, detracts from the beauty of the game. Youth play must be based upon individual technical ability, creativity, and the smarts to figure out where and what to do on the field according to the circumstances of play. The decision-making capacity to play one's position, or a teammate's if required, must result from a player's wits and acumen, the development of which is a lesson that goes beyond soccer.

12. No Cancellations

At the information meeting for parents before the start of the fall soccer season in Italy, the coach of my son's team gave a short, welcoming introduction about plans and hopes for the season. He handed out the schedule and well-worn club uniforms, at least in their fifth year of use. (At the end of the season, the uniforms would again be returned for next year's squad.)

To my surprise, the coach's talk focused on the post-practice shower. Some Italian localities can be fussy about having everyone take a shower after practice. There is also a practical side here. If the kid takes a shower at the locker room, then participation in sport does not impinge on the family water-heating bill. The choice of showers as the main topic was puzzling. I thought we would be talking soccer.

When the coach opened the floor to questions, I raised my hand to ask, "How will you let us know when practice is canceled."

I did not understand why the other parents had not brought up what I thought would be a main topic of discussion. I expected the coach to respond that they would send a text message or an email. Instead, the other parents turned around and looked at me. When they realized I was the American, they regarded me not with unkindness or disdain, but quizzically, as if to say, "How on earth did that country ever win World War II?"

The coach answered without hesitation, "We never cancel practice." Then everyone in the room acted as if I had never said anything.

Luckily, before asking something else foolish like, "What about rain or snow?" I realized that, like taking showers, my question was due to cultural conditioning. I had not even asked "if" practice was to be canceled, but "when," as if canceling practice was not a hypothetical possibility, but a certainty.

Many Italian towns were laid out on a grid by the ancient Romans. The playing fields established by the local administration for my son's team were within walking distance for most participants. Questions of liability for car accidents did not exist. If there were a real calamity, an earthquake or a flood, then practice would not take place for obvious reasons. At the time, Italy did not have a culture of public announcement and media frenzy over cancellations. No rush to the morning television or social media to check if school was canceled after a dusting of snow or a morning fog. When activities are canceled, citizens are more likely to be involved in a collective effort to stem the effects of the calamity than to be thinking about a sporting event or even school.

In the United States, sports and school are canceled more often for reasons having to do with perceived legal liability than for hurricanes, floods, earthquakes, or wildfires. This rush to cancel has spread to all aspects of organized activity, with the neurotic and even hysterical reporting of the American news media trying to increase viewership with warnings about an approaching storm.

The Italian coach and parents lived in a culture where soccer practices or games are canceled only according to FIFA guidelines—when there is enough water, mud, ice, or snow that a ball dropped on the field lands with a thud rather than bouncing skyward. On such occasions, practices and games move to a covered structure, if available. Along with the showers and locker rooms, many Italian communes also have covered artificial turf fields or basketball/tennis courts under a canvas bubble. The indoor practices were beehives of activity like those described in the "No Space" chapter. A little city planning had rendered any question of cancellations moot.

To be fair, we were in an Alpine region where the major local sports were not soccer but mountain running, skiing, and cycling. When locals hesitate about doing something because of the rain or snow, the standard retort is "Are you made of sugar?"

Had I been foolish enough to ask the coach what happens if it rains, he likely would have answered, "We'll get wet."

After the meeting, I approached the coach to explain my question. In America, games and practices were often canceled, the *pratomania* (obsession with fields) described in the "No Grass" chapter.

One of the parents, a bon vivant-wisecracker chipped in jokingly, "No wonder America sucks at the game." The jab had an element of truth. If Americans often canceled games and practices out of fear of the weather and lawyers or because grass fields were considered more important than children, then how could the country ever catch up with the rest of the world?

That season when it did rain, the kids played on a part of the field set aside for such occasions, instead of on the lined game field. The team's practice was interrupted and canceled just once that season when an Alpine rescue helicopter landed on the field to organize a search party for a lost German hiker. Hiking in the Alps is risky, but so is being alive. If hiking off-trail were made illegal, such a law would be unenforceable. Societies decide which risks they are willing to accept.

Lawyer Insurance

An excuse for American readiness to cancel events is that the United States is a litigious society. The running joke is that in some areas of the country, usually California, people needing money think more about who to sue than about how to land a job.

Many of the founding fathers of the nation were lawyers. Their legal expertise afforded Americans the brilliant advantages from the US Constitution and Bill of Rights, enshrined the freedoms to "pursue happiness," and limited how government and corporations can impinge on our lives. However, life in a society created by and for lawyers also means that parks and rec departments and clubs justifiably fear lawsuits charging negligence in protecting children from arguably avoidable distress or injury. People who run soccer clubs are in the business of providing venues for sport, not wallowing in lawsuits. The result is that most activities in the United States exist under the burden of insurance requirements and legal waivers, making excessive cancellations the norm rather than the exception.

When the practice or game of a parks and rec league or club team are inexplicably canceled, parents under the impetus to "helicopter" their children may naïvely think about organizing a pickup game at the local school or church gym. However, they are usually turned away. The near entirety of such venues in the United States have draconian restrictions due to insurance contracts that do not cover injury or mishap to extraneous participants, not to mention the deductible payment before any reimbursement for damages may be claimed and received.

At times, soccer players in the US may feel an affinity with the skateboarder's lament, "Skateboarding is not a crime." Wanting to kick a ball around with some friends should also not be a crime, but perhaps excessive cancellations of games, practice, and school should be. As with other examples in this book, it is a question of culture. The after-practice shower was part of the cultural conditioning of the coach in this chapter's opening anecdote, but canceling a game or practice was not. In contrast, whether to cancel or not is often the first question in America, where the cost of maintaining grass fields and the fear of litigation often trumps the interests of children.

The solution here is, of course, to reform our overly litigious society.

Just kidding.

There are multiple aspects of American culture that we cannot pretend to resolve or even mention in a book on how to fix youth soccer. Yet, the ideas herein could have wider applications. The simple truth is that keeping soccer a much more local, low-key affair will require fewer functionaries, policies, guidelines, and bylaws. The more basic the playing field, like a blacktop, the less likely are concerns about the protections and safety measures those fields require. Low-key, free-play soccer requires less official or parental intervention, and thus, the more likely it is that it will be a limited and simple affair not subject to contingencies requiring cancellations, insurance claims, or lawsuits.

In today's American culture, liability forms will still be necessary. But even the most litigious locales can be rendered harmless with an iron-clad liability release form covering games being played at the school, blacktop, or the center down the street. In the low-stress system we're proposing, lawyers will have to find business elsewhere. Or they can take off their shoes and join in the match, after they sign the waiver.

13. No Hands

KTG

A ten-year-old boy who had grown up playing street ball in Europe was the new kid in school. After navigating the new language in the classroom, he was looking forward to recess. He thought the other kids might come to respect him as a fair soccer player so he could make some friends.

To his surprise, at recess the boys were not playing soccer, or even American football, basketball, or baseball but something they called *smear the queer,* later also known as "muckle ball" or "kill the guy" (KTG). In the game each player tries to hold on to the ball for as long as possible before being tackled and having the ball ripped away. The result is a horde of scrums, pileups, and intense grabbing until the ball flips out and some other brave soul runs away with it to bask momentarily in the spotlight.

The game may seem idiotic, a bunch of kids fighting over a ball with no score or rules. KTG is a primitive, cheap game that requires little or no organization, has few rules, and needs no equipment. If a ball is not handy, almost any object will do. Nobody wins or loses in a game of KTG unless players are organized into teams on a field with goal lines at either end, in which case the game becomes like Rugby.

KTG has much in common with the desire for kids playing street soccer around the world to hog the ball and to fake out everyone on the field, a feat which rarely, if ever, results in a goal. KTG and street soccer tap into the basic, primitive vestiges of play that predate anything civilized, perhaps even language. Any kid witnessing a game of KTG or street soccer does not need someone to explain the idea behind the game: get the ball. The difference between KTG and street soccer is catching and carrying the ball versus kicking and dribbling it, but the universal impulse of children to play is the same.

No Justice, No Dribble

The US is the country of great inventions, of labor-saving devices that emphasize what the brain can command the hands to do. The etymology of the word "artificial" is from the Latin for "handicraft," what can be made with the hands, which offers an analogy in American sports tradition. Just think of the intricacies of the various baseball pitches for the fingers to produce a curve ball or a slider. There are manual techniques for proper placement of the hands on the basketball or on an American football, requiring precise hand-to-eye coordination.

Soccer teaches a different mentality in early learning stages due to the predominance of the feet over the hands. The essential feature of soccer and the difficulty of controlling the ball with the feet make the game harder to predict.

Soccer may seem to run contrary to Superman's motto, "Truth, justice, and the American way." The truth that one team is superior to another will not necessarily result in the justice of an expected result. In soccer, the "American way" of ensuring outcomes through the artifice of equipment, planning, and wealth cannot guarantee victory. American culture favors the optimism to believe in solutions to solve problems.

The unpredictability, the seeming unfairness of soccer is precisely the essence of its charm and appeal. Soccer, like life, has destinies, slings and arrows, that can be difficult, if not impossible, to predict. One can prepare to a certain extent. But when reality rears its head, one must also be able to improvise. Maybe the expression, *to think quickly on your feet,* was coined by a soccer-playing Englishman or Scot. The attempt to control life can impede learning in a sport like soccer which has, at its essence, the primitive chaos, unpredictability, and irrationality of KTG.

Girth, Adaptability, and Hierarchy

The emphasis on physicality in American football and basketball has carried over into the American style of soccer and particularly in the high school and college game in the form of unlimited substitutions. A soccer commonplace is that NCAA Division-III games offer a better spectacle than the NCAA Division-I game due to the latter's emphasis on size, strength, and speed. In soccer, height or girth is not necessarily an advantage. The greatest forwards of all time were uniformly short. Pele is five feet eight inches tall, Messi five feet six. Being tall means having to stoop over to play a ball, which is usually on the ground.

Nor were these great players heavy. The best American player at the writing of this chapter, Christian Pulisic, has a weight listed at 139 pounds. This isn't to say that size and strength are necessarily a disadvantage either. Gerard Pique is six foot four, Zlatan Ibrahimović is six foot five, and Peter Crouch is six foot seven! The point is that soccer does not require a certain physical type. Part of the game's vast appeal is that anyone can play.

The American sporting emphasis on physicality extends to the macho, or masochistic mantras of "no pain, no gain" or "taking one for the team." It is as if American sports were the heirs of the ancient Roman gladiator games which originated as human-sacrifice rituals where two slaves fought to the death. The fallacy of the sacrificial element in American sport may be countered by a line from the film, *Patton* (1970). In one scene, actor George C. Scott as WWII American General George S. Patton (1885-1945) addresses the troops, cynically haranguing that, "The point of war is not to die for your country, but to make the other son-of-a-bitch die for his." In soccer, the team that runs and hustles the most, that works the most, does not necessarily win. The team that wins is the one that correctly applies its efforts and abilities to the circumstances at hand.

Most sports have military origins. Bored soldiers in the barracks betting on who could throw a cannon ball the farthest invented the track and field event called the shot put. There are similar origins to the javelin and even foot races. As mentioned before, soccer has grisly origins as a celebratory ritual of soldiers kicking around something in a bag, like the head of a vanquished foe. KTG probably has similar origins, although instead of kicking the object, the soldiers carried the object, and tackled each other to get it. Both these games occurred in moments in military life as a respite from the discipline of obeying orders, in moments of freedom from hierarchy. The DNA of soccer, like KTG, arises from this release from hierarchical control.

Traditional American sports, in contrast, are hierarchical, more like preparation maneuvers for the battles soldiers fight as a unit. Baseball gained in popularity during the American Civil War 1861-1865 and has a structure that replicates much of the division of labor that occurs within an army, particularly in terms of waiting around for orders. American football is the most hierarchical sport of all, originating as an offshoot of the English catch-and-carry game, Rugby. The game developed in the late twentieth century with extreme specialization among players. Comedian George Carlin riffed that in American football the game is under the direction of a "field general" quarterback, who directs his forces in a coordinated ground and aerial assault.

Position names in American football indicate both role and placement on the field: linesman, center, halfback, fullback, safety, linebacker, and so on. There is similar nomenclature for soccer positions where jersey number indicates role and field position. The number one was for the goalie and number nine for the center forward. This has changed in the modern game, as the British heritage waned. Soccer players still understand the identification of number with position. But as the game has sped up and the ball has become lighter, players must think (on their feet) about where to go and what to do. In soccer, players must also be aware of, and adapt to, tactical changes within the course of a game. They cannot always rely on the intervention of a coach who cannot stop the game with a time out and who is limited to three substitutions.

American sports also feature the added intrusion of the clock, forcing players to shoot the basketball or hike the football within a set amount of time. These clocks add a further organizational and administrative layer to the game. Kids on a playground cannot set up and enforce play according to a clock, nor should they have to. The stoppage of time removes initiative from the individual players, many of whom in American football can get through a game without making a single strategic decision on their own. In this vein, the idea of replacing the players in American football with robots, as featured on one network's NFL marketing, does not seem farfetched.

Soccer players receive criticism for diving and faking injuries to waste time or to provoke irrational reactions and even the expulsion of opponents. There is a seeming anarchy in soccer, which is part of the charm of the game. One referee, aided by two linesmen, must manage twenty-two players on a field longer and wider than the field of American football. Fans of American football, accustomed to nearly unlimited possibilities to stop play, may not understand, but this is why soccer players have to be able to think on their feet. Would it be too cynical to suggest that American sports are games for lawyers or armchair generals?

Exceptionalism?

America considers itself an exceptional country. But what nation does not consider itself exceptional? In soccer, the English considered themselves so exceptional that they refused to compete in international competitions. Then in the 1950 World Cup, irony of ironies, they were beaten 1-0 by a team of Americans, many of whom were foreign-born amateurs.[1]

The word "exceptional" has two different connotations indicating either inferiority or superiority. America's traditional team sports are exceptional in that they are separate and not practiced globally at the universal level of soccer. That is fine. Those sports, like many others, are there to be enjoyed by those who love them. Currently, American soccer is not exceptional under the notion of excellence, but of inferiority. The first step to address this reality is to accept it as the truth, to understand why traditional American sports do not prepare children to compete with the rest of the world. Once we recognize this deficiency and accept the challenge, then Americans can put their talents and spirit into solving the problem.

Let It Be Girls

At a Montessori school-wide project, children made "peace sticks," carefully and lovingly decorated in art class before a group photo outside. There, to the dismay of the teachers, the boys realized the "peace sticks" made excellent swords and began to whack each other in pretend duels. Meanwhile, the girls peacefully cooperated, building houses and commenting on each other's peace-stick handiwork. There was no hitting. At early ages, boys and girls often express different interests in play.

When playing tackle football was permissible in American public schools, KTG was almost an exclusively boy's affair. Not that girls were not allowed, but given the rules of the game, they were understandably uninterested. The impulse to hog the ball for a few seconds of glory before being tackled by a mob lacked inter-gender appeal. A chaotic, almost rule-free game like KTG prizes irrational individuality and risk taking. The object of the game is not to win by scoring points, but to enjoy the thrill of a brief moment of glory. For a young boy, that free-for-all moment clenching the ball, avoiding being tackled down for the inevitable scrum with all hands trying to pry the ball loose is pure sporting pleasure. In street soccer, instead of carrying the ball like an American football running back in KTG, kids dribble and fake and run with the ball at their feet for a few seconds like a star striker. That cauldron of KTG-like, street-soccer unpredictability is precisely what the sterile environment of American soccer culture lacks.

But wait. Not all Americans have been humiliated in international soccer competition. The US women's team has won three of the World Cups played since 1991. Perhaps the current US system with opportunities for orderly socialization and controlled learning have benefits as demonstrated by the success of the American female game? So why all the fuss about individuality, creativity, and *shoeless soccer*?

American women have enjoyed success because other countries have not fully developed their female soccer cultures. While American boys were (and still are) playing catch-up to the rest of the world, the girls were at the vanguard. Where do seventeen year-old girls in Argentina, Italy, or Spain go to play, if they play at all? Until very recently, neither of us had ever seen a girls' soccer game anywhere in Argentina, Italy, or Spain. We know of course that they must have existed, but we had still never seen any, anywhere.

There have been twenty World Cup men's finals and a team from either Argentina or Italy played in half of them. There have been eight women's World Cup finals with the US team playing in half of them. By that measure American women are the best in the world. The quick explanation is that in contrast to Italy and Argentina, practically as many American girls play as boys. American girls also enjoy the advantage of Title IX requirements for equal numbers of players in genders in college athletic programs. Since American football teams require so many players on the roster due to limitless substitutions, some collegiate male team sports were eliminated, and women's sports programs such as soccer were funded. In many soccer-playing nations like Argentina and Italy, which lack high school or college athletics, such opportunities for women do not exist.

Recent challenges to US women's supremacy in international competition indicate that the rest of the world may be catching up, as traditional powers and newcomers realize that soccer is not only for the boys. The American women's game is nowhere near the state of crisis of the men's game internationally. However, in comparison to peers worldwide, neither American boys nor girls for the most part can vaunt the kind of mindless cultural affinity with the game, the KTG, street soccer foundation that is the belly feeding a grassroots national soccer culture. This lack of a cultural foundation forebodes poorly for both men's and the women's game.

So what to do? Again, there are long-term, cultural benefits to reducing the outer trappings of the US soccer system (the fields, shoes, travel, uniforms, balls) for replacement with opportunities to learn how to play in those small-space, hard-court, shoeless, multi-age soccer games at the heart of the *shoeless soccer* approach.

We do not want to dismantle successful female soccer programs, nor devalue the social aspects of the club scene that many children enjoy. Instead, we want to point out the advantages to learning the game with a less-is-more approach. If we can awaken the individuality and creativity perhaps dormant in both the American girls' and boys' game, then the future is ours.

Why not dream big? Rather than resting on laurels, the US women's game could take the sport to the next level by developing such quality that the female game could enjoy spectatorship not limited to the four-year World Cup cycle. People could start to watch the women's game not just because it is the World Cup, but because women, and American women in particular, play not only great team soccer but have even developed the individual flair typically associated with the Peles and Maradonas of men's soccer. The US can thus live up to its reputation for exceptionalism by raising the level of not just its men's game, but of its already world-class women's game, establishing a truly sustainable women's game, not just for the US, but for the world.

14. No Quidditch

On a frigid Midwest evening, wind chill was not so much about temperature as about how the water in your eyes might freeze when walking in the direction of the howling westerly gusts sweeping off the plain.

Members of the International Football Club, a student organization at the local university, trudged through the snow from their dorms to play a pick-up game of soccer in the indoor turf room. The grass on the full-sized American football field was not real, but it was green. The indoor temperature setting of 68 degrees Fahrenheit meant that one could run and even build up a sweat, momentarily forgetting the bitter cold outside.

Then, at the reception desk bad news, very bad news: "The university Quidditch team has the turf room."

"What's Quidditch?"

The club members, who hailed from every part of the globe, peered into the field house where about ten students were running around with broomsticks between their legs throwing a ball into a horizontal basketball hoop.

Then they looked at me, the faculty advisor who had been helping the International Football Club presidents and treasurers organize these games for over a decade. Every fall, the elected club leaders sent out an email inviting international student groups to pickup games. A few came, then the word would spread that there was a group playing soccer at a good level, and the numbers would swell. The rules were simple. If someone thought they had been fouled, then play stopped. Giving everyone the right to call a foul paradoxically reduced fouling. No slide tackles on 50-50 balls. Teams were divided by light shirts versus dark shirts. When the pickup games moved outdoors, play continued until late evening when it was too dark to see the ball.

After a year of unexpected cancellations and botched reservation confirmations, the Quidditch scheduling mix-up was the last straw. As faculty advisor, I had failed to understand that a university club had to be officially approved, with all the required liability forms and by-laws (whatever those are). We had not understood that we needed signed contract agreements and membership lists double-checked by the facilities office. Without the paperwork, Quidditch took over.

After the club leaders filled out the forms and I signed them, the university dutifully funded the group, which then received internally accounted fees which we signed over to reserve the turf room. With excess funds, the club bought portable goals, pinnies, and balls (none of which were really needed). Then the problem became what to do with the excess money. The International Football Club always seemed to end the year with a surplus. Soccer is the poor man's sport, a player's game. Equipment gets in the way.

The level of play in the club was high since the international students had learned the game about the time they had learned to brush their teeth. When the university varsity had a bad year, the coach would invite the fitter players to scrimmage. Some joined the varsity to play NCAA Division-I soccer and commented that the physical training was far more than they had expected.

University admissions determined the composition of the participants of the International Football Club. Foreign exchange students tended to follow one another, encouraged by agreements between administrations for scholarship opportunities or the fluctuating exchange rate of the US dollar. One period, there had been a sizable cohort of students from Saudi Arabia. Other years, there had been numerous students from sub-Saharan Africa. There had been years of an exchange with a French business school and with a Brazilian supply-chain management program.

Soccer is the world's game. There was no better evidence of its universality than twenty, thirty, even forty international students, plus a smattering of Americans, playing, laughing, teasing each other, and enjoying being alive. The members did not really keep score in the games but changed the composition of teams if the goal count became lopsided. What members sought was not really victory but recognition for a remarkable or beautiful play, whether as the fruit of individual brilliance or team chemistry, the kind of sports action on highlight films reported in game summaries. When such an event occurred, the members of the club applauded, even for a play by the opposing team.

So many nations had provided members to the club over the years, from Kazakhstan to Argentina, that at times there could be ten, even twenty, different languages spoken, not to mention the different variants of imperial Castilian, English, and French.

National stereotypes among club members came out in individual style of play. The Brazilians, who were supposed to be the most joyous, often seemed burdened by their reputation as the world's best. There was a streak of unpredictable physicality in the play of Central Americans. When there were enough Chinese players, they grouped together and commanded organization. The odd British players earned the nickname, "The Empire Strikes Back," for their impetus to head the ball like "mad dogs and Englishmen." Some of the Eastern Europeans, like the Bulgarians, held true to a macho intensity. The Germans, Austrians, and Slavs were proficient, the Spaniards vibrant, and the Italians calculating. The South Americans shared a propensity with the Dutch to play straight at the opposing goal. When there were enough sub-Saharan Africans, one could discern differences between the playing styles of Kenyans, Cameroonians, Ghanaians, or Malians. The same could be said of Middle Easterners, who revealed a certain reticence in assigning culpability regarding the rules but never made any fuss about women playing with the group, although such practice might have been anathema to radical theocratic currents in their some of their cultures. The Americans, who came with shin guards and booted the ball downfield, adapted to the style of play and often made lifelong friends among the international students, who were no longer foreigners, but "those guys I play ball with." Differences between tenured faculty and janitorial staff were irrelevant. One could quickly perceive which players had no formal coaching because they tried to fake out the entire opposing team by themselves, rather than thinking about a smart pass or assist.

The differences between the members of the club were not a source of contention, but an expression of individuality. The games revealed an optimistic possibility for humanity to live in harmony, to play together, to enjoy what the Spaniards call *la fiesta del fútbol* (the celebration of football.) The pickup games were like the Coca Cola commercial song, "I'd Like to Teach the World to Sing," or the "We Are the World," USA for Africa benefit song. There were occasional scrapes and personality conflicts, but nothing to destroy the universal spirit of the game.

Soccer Stereotypes

Quidditch is a fantasy game that is difficult to play since none of us are witches or wizards with wands and broomsticks. Quidditch, as described in the *Harry Potter* novels, also makes little sense since the object of play is to get the *golden snitch,* a play which renders the rest of the game redundant.

In contrast to Quidditch, soccer is not a fantasy. National identities reflect in how different peoples play the game. The Brazilian game is founded on barefooted beach and urban play with creativity stemming from African roots and Portuguese verve, the *jogo bonito*, the beautiful game.

The German game, *fussball,* relied on organization and discipline. This held until embarrassment at the group stages of the 2000 European Cup provoked a retooling concentrating at the youth academy level, even if recent German international success may actually be a result of the street ball influences from the country's recent immigrant influx. The Italian game, the *catenaccio* (the chain), is based on the ancient geographical reality of a peninsula whose inhabitants often face better-armed and organized invaders (usually Germans, but also French, Spaniards, and most recently Americans). The Italian game takes nothing for granted, employing tactics that strive to squeak out advantages through cunning and technical ability. Like medieval hill-town defenders who bicker amongst themselves about whether it is better to surrender or unify and risk the wrath of the invader, Italy tends to win the World Cup when the players' personal interests are at stake. Italy won the World Cup in 1982 and 2006 when, coincidentally, players sought to clear their reputations after game-fixing scandals.

The Hispanic game has many variants, from Catalonia to Argentina. The tenor of the Hispanic game derives from the reputation of Spaniards as the best individual soldiers during the sixteenth-century with the pride to take on opponents and to sacrifice for God and King. This prideful impetus derives from what Argentinians call the *enganche,* the bold move of a skillful player like Maradona or Messi to lead and inspire the attack. When Catalan organization and the technical ability of the *tiki taka,* quick-pass game combined with Castilian imperial drive, Spain vaunted a winning style of football.

The spirit of the Dutch game, total football, is often explained as a reaction to a geography that must be wrested from a hostile nature with the ever-present risk of flooding, requiring adeptness from all. Iceland has made a strength out of their small population, fostering a sense of identity in unity and team spirit with world-class instruction. The French were a constant also-ran in world football until immigration brought the technical vibrancy and communal aspect of African football with its flashy build-ups and booming pace.

This brings us to the paradox of the accredited inventors of the game, the English. The English kick-and-chase game played on the muddy, grass fields of Eaton demanded speed, size, and strength. However, the sailors of the British Empire, who played barefooted in tight spaces on the decks of ships or ports of call, brought the game to the world. The latter is the game that has become the number-one sport on the globe, leaving the British game behind. Unfortunately, as noted in previous chapters, the former style continues to dominate the culture of US soccer.[1]

America's Colonial Soccer Identity

The countries and cultures above have a sense of their soccer DNA as the foundation of their national federations' organizational strategies and individual style of play. What about America and an American style of play for an American soccer identity?

America has always considered itself unbound by the shackles of the Old World and has felt certain of its ability to overcome adversity, accept and overcome a challenge, to put a man on the moon. So how can a country that has led the world with so many inventions and innovations be so bad at the world's game?

The American sports of baseball, American football, and basketball are catch-and-throw games. Association football, soccer, is a kick-the-ball game, not traditionally rooted in American culture. Therefore, American soccer identity must be defined and promoted to debunk the notion that America's very exceptionalism requires a separate sporting culture, which is an update of the British "we are too good to play with you" foolishness that kept UK teams out of international competition until 1950.[2]

While it's true that we've made plenty of references to how soccer is played in other parts of the world, the point is not to copy their models or their styles. The US is not Brazil, Germany, or Spain. US Soccer should apply an American solution based upon American cultural strengths for a narrative of can-do football based on American know-how. American soccer culture must be something we can believe in and in which we can invest time, effort, treasure, and, our most important asset, our children. America's present soccer crisis would seem like a made-to-order opportunity for the application of American can-do and know-how, to a complex task. If we do not succeed, at least we will have tried and can be proud of our efforts.

So what is the basis for America's footballing identity?

The country was founded to free herself of English rule over two hundred years ago. Ironically, English style still infects American soccer. From youth play to the MLS, it is difficult to find an indigenous game uncontaminated by the kick-and-chase of nineteenth-century, English-style football. The American men's national team that could not beat Trinidad and Tobago to qualify for the 2018 World Cup had much in common in terms of style of play with the English side eliminated by Iceland in the 2014 World Cup. To this day, American youth players selected for elite coaching often end up in the charge of an Englishman, or at best a Scot, as if the American soccer system is particularly susceptible to the Old World charm of a British accent. After all, it is their language. They speak English better than Americans, whose enjoyment of its lily tones evokes the prejudice that the speaker is also competent.

To their credit, the English have taken cultural material from America and transformed it through the grit of that same charm. Howling Wolf may be among the greatest bluesmen of all time. Yet, with Jimmy Page and Robert

Plant of Led Zeppelin, Howling Wolf's songs became something else (just listen to the Zeppelin cover of Howling Wolf's song "Killing Floor.")

Unfortunately, in soccer, the British have not been as innovative as in music. British coaches might not even be conscious of transmitting an idea of the game at the cutting edge of the 1890s. Yet, they cannot help but emit the culture of the kick-and-chase English game because in the US, as in Britain, the game is played mainly on grass fields. This substructure creates a superstructure favoring the unskilled melee of English-style kick-and-chase football. This is not to suggest that all English coaches should be proscribed from coaching in America, but they should be treated with suspicion.

An American Soccer Uprising

The time has come for an American uprising in soccer to develop a can-do style that breaks the vestiges of British colonialism. There is no better place to define what is fundamentally American than with the founding document of American identity, the Declaration of Independence, and its key phrase, "life, liberty, and the pursuit of happiness."

Thomas Jefferson took the phrase from English philosopher John Locke's ideas about life, liberty, and property, which proposes property, or wealth and belongings, as a goal in human endeavor. Of course, wealth and property come in very handy. Anyone without wealth or property will think that obtaining some wealth and property affords a path to happiness. The wealthiest people are not necessarily the happiest, nor even happier than their less-wealthy fellow citizens. The American soccer fans who witnessed the wealthiest country in the world humiliated by Panama and by Trinidad and Tobago in 2018 World Cup qualifying were certainly not happy. America's wealth, its pristine fields and expensive equipment and coaching, did not lead to success or, in the case of World Cup qualifying, even to a sense of dignity.

Wealth has diminishing returns. Once basic needs are met, with what economists call inelastic goods, the ones you cannot bend, then adding goods, the elastic goods, increases happiness only marginally, if at all. A child without food will starve. A child who eats too much food will become obese. A child with one toy will treasure it. A child with hundreds of toys will become bored with most of them. A child who learns to play adorned with the accoutrements of a professional player but lacks basic spontaneous, unconsciously competent ability with the ball is being cheated out of the true joy in playing the game. Skill and creativity cannot be replaced with "stuff."

Jefferson replaced Locke's "property" with the phrase "the pursuit of happiness" because activity and the quest for solutions render people happy. Some of the most miserable people are lottery winners, whose newfound riches ablate them from their previous identities, the goals and efforts that gave their lives meaning. To paraphrase the entire Arthurian cycle, every novel by Tolkien, and even Dante's *Divine Comedy,* the quest is the thing.

Jefferson probably did not play a lot of shoeless soccer.[3] However, Jefferson did understand that happiness lies in the pursuit, the dream, the invention needed to reach a goal. Jefferson achieved many goals in his life from remarkable inventions to the founding and designing of the grounds of the University of Virginia. He did so by recognizing genius and adapting its lessons to his own conditions. Jefferson's plans for the grounds of the University of Virginia and his home Monticello were inspired by the work of architect Andrea Palladio, who, in turn, applied the lessons of ancient Romans like Vitruvius. However, Jefferson's architecture is not a carbon copy of Palladio or Vitruvius. Jefferson's architecture adapts brilliant influences to a local setting. The same strategy could apply to solutions for fixing US soccer. The individual pursuit of happiness is what has guided this country. In terms of teaching soccer to children, the key word here is "individual," and the pursuit of the skills and creativity of the beautiful game.

The other ingenious and indigenous document of America's founding is the Bill of Rights by Jefferson's neighbor and fellow planter-class aristocrat, James Madison. The Bill of Rights is a list of what an English King and, by extension, any government may not do to a citizen. Madison begins his list of freedoms with the phrase, "Congress shall make no law" before tearing into the list of liberties still contested and infringed upon by governments around the world, including our own. Most people are not rich planter-aristocrats, yet this libertarian delight in freedom, the right to do your own thing, enshrined in the Bill of Rights, is a universal human drive.

The "beautiful" part of the beautiful game is the creativity that results from the freedom to learn and to play without constraint or supervision, without the intrusion of unlimited player substitutions, which devalue player initiative. There is a paradox about soccer where less-is-more, where wealth and means may become a hindrance, where structure and organization hamper creativity. Like the Declaration of Independence, soccer replaces property with the pursuit of happiness. Like the Bill of Rights, soccer rewards the individualism and invitation to creativity that is the currency of the freedoms in Madison's brilliant list. In the tradition of the Declaration of Independence and the Bill of Rights, soccer must be thought of as the most American of games for championing the quest for life's goals and the freedom to enact one's own ideas.

So what about the question of America's cultural identity as reflected in a style of play? Historically Brazilians are the best at creativity and grace. Italians are the best at defense. Germans are the best at organization.

The Dutch are the best at teamwork. Hispanics are the best at heroic initiative (and Catalans best at organizing the Hispanic character thereby). At what should the Americans become the best? What should be the identifying characteristic of an American style of play?

We could return to the idea of the country as a melting pot where everything comes together to make a strong union as in the Latin inscription on American coinage, *e pluribus unum* (out of many one). One approach would be to propose that US soccer should aim to be the best at everything. This approach has been tried before with limited success by nations such as Russia, Japan, and now China. These nations have often focused on top-down, organized training without recognizing that, before any coaching is effective, the essential skills of the game must be in place as spontaneous, cultural elements from below, as automatic as hitting a light switch. A third, perhaps more cynical option, would be to argue that America's approach has always been one of might and power—a kind of shock-and-awe approach to conquering world football that would recall the American military's reliance on air power. But we've already seen, time and again in this book, how the big, strong, and fast do not always carry the day in soccer.

America is many things: a melting pot, an exceptional nation, and, of course, over much of the last century, the most powerful nation on the planet. Yet, America's essence remains enshrined in its founding documents. We are people who declare our independence, who set out into the wilderness in search of freedom and opportunity, who explore and remake ourselves, who tinker in garages, fixing our automobiles or building personal computers from bit parts. Except for the poverty, we are the essence of street soccer. A lack of poverty should not paradoxically be a handicap. Indeed, we must insist with all the resources at our disposal that the money changers in America's sports industrial complex must leave us alone so our libertarian, frontier-thesis, Bill-of-Rights approach to life can express itself. Our kids need to be free to overcome the paradoxical disadvantages posed by manicured lawns, ideal spaces, shoes, regulation balls, shin guards, deep benches, coaches, referees, and helicopter parents.

American children should learn to play barefooted, on hard surfaces, in limited space to become more creative than Brazilians. Americans should be more defensive stalwarts than the Italians, defending the goal with grit and a presumption of impenetrability learned from playing barefooted with hyperinflated balls. Americans should organize a coaching curriculum from the best in the world, maybe from Iceland, so that knowledge of the game is widespread enough to allow Americans to tinker with the game and unleash our inventive genius. Americans should stay at home, playing, instead of doing drills. There should be game after game with entire neighborhoods of kids who stay together and mix regularly with older and younger kids in low-intensity contests where daring and creativity, the pursuit of happiness, are not censured. Then any American who wishes to play the game as a pastime may do so with a sense of pride in their abilities and in their soccer culture, without envying people who grew up in "soccer-playing" countries. Americans should harness their initiative and face challenges in accordance with the drive and resilience of a nation that produced Edison, Ford, the Wright Brothers, the personal computer, the internet, and privately funded space travel.

Then, maybe the US men's national team will be able to defeat a team of second-stringers representing Trinidad and Tobago in a half-empty stadium and qualify for a World Cup.

But more importantly, American children will thrive in a system where less-is-more. Where parents can be supporters rather than helicopter pilots. Where coaches are free to teach the game rather than to worry about collecting trophies of dubious value. Where, after years of local play, earning a spot on the roster of a developmental academy is a reward, both emotional and financial, for real ability and skill rather than an indication of the ability to pay or drive to distant practices. Then American children can experience what is truly "fun," which is to be good at something, to enjoy the fruits of labor as an expression of their individual spirit and character.

15. No Complex

When Scott was seven-years-old, he lived in Southern California, an American soccer "hotbed" that produced US men's national team players. Like them, Scott signed up for soccer. So far, so good. Scott, now aged thirty, still plays in adult leagues as well as in once-a-week pickup games. Scott's love for the beautiful game inspired him to coach youth teams while in college, and now his own children play. So is Scott an American soccer success story?

Unfortunately, he is yet another American soccer tragedy. Scott started in the system but he didn't last. By age twelve, he was fed up and quit.

What turned him off from soccer? Standing in lines, waiting to dribble through cones, listening to coaches talk, talk, and then talk some more while he and the rest of the kids stood around listening and bored. From those coaches Scott learned that soccer is a game where you kick the stuffing out of a ball and then chase down the field.

Today Scott recalls the whole experience as utterly pointless, a tragic waste of his talents.

Afterward, Scott turned to basketball, then running, swimming, and surfing. He had a nice, pleasant childhood.

But when it comes to soccer, he feels shortchanged.

After his freshmen year in college, Scott spent a couple of years in South America. There, he accidently rediscovered what the American soccer system had denied him. For Scott the game people there called *fútbol* was love at first sight. This *fútbol* had precision passing, constant movement, fluid teamwork, achingly beautiful angles, genius runs, and almost inexplicable goals. It was the beautiful game.

But while his discovery was, for him, a cause to rejoice, he also re-experienced feelings of anger and disappointment about his US youth soccer experience. He was even angrier because he realized he had been ripped off by a system without quality control and hence without quality. He was bitter at having spent half a decade learning almost nothing and then walking away from what, he realized, was the most beautiful game he'd ever played.

But what does Scott have to do with the failure of the US men's national team? That's the question pundits might consider if they were to read this. Except, they probably won't read, and likely won't ask. Maybe they don't really care. From our perspective, observing and coaching soccer at the grassroots level for a combined several decades, those in charge appear interested only in soccer at a certain level, which was not Scott's grassroots level. Which brings us back to explaining how Scott's experience determined the failure of the US men's national team.

Scott didn't have parents who understood the system. They didn't know not to sign him up for Southern California AYSO soccer rec league from the get-go. Once he was in AYSO, like most kids at his level he was randomly placed with mediocre coaches, and he never developed. Consequently, no one ever identified him as having anything special. No one informed his parents about other opportunities, and he was left behind.

So what, the same pundits might ask? Southern California in those years still produced former US men's national team players like Maurice Edu and Steve Birnbaum, as well as Landon Donovan a few years earlier. Plus Scott did not have the athleticism to overcome poor coaching. If we went to see him play today we would see an average player. Scott, in fact, would be the first to admit that he is a good but not great athlete. So why was losing him a problem?

In those years what Southern California produced wasn't good enough, even if limiting discussion to elite players. Where did the players who rose out of Southern California soccer get us? Certainly not to the 2018 World

Cup in Russia. They did not get us there for a myriad of reasons. But the simplest explanation is lack of quality. Why did they lack quality? Again, myriad reasons. But there's an obvious one that few appear to address either because they don't understand it or see it as somehow insurmountable. Namely that the US isn't a soccer nation. We don't have the culture.

It's *Not* in the Water

We don't disagree. But, so what? Is culture somehow magic? A mystical entity comprised of a secret combination of Latin genes, Germanic linguistics, and Italian urban planning? The other guys have it and we don't. We're screwed. Let's go home.

Brazil is a "soccer culture," they say. So too are Spain, Italy, England, and Argentina. But the USA, well, just isn't. With those convenient excuses, the powers that be are free to keep working to build better mousetraps, throwing money, uniforms, and costly infrastructure at a problem of their own making. Moreover, with such a simplistic notion of culture, the mousetraps they design are ironically what we might call "countercultural," in the worst sense. They are not designed for the people who live in the culture, not for the *common, ordinary, soccer-playing American* (in other words, the rest of us, not to mention our kids). Instead, the system is for a handful of elite athletes who have been blessed with genes that allow them to survive or transcend the culture.

The system is designed for a handful of elite athletes who happened to take a liking to soccer, plus the kids whose parents are lucky enough to know the game and have the knowledge and resources to navigate the system. Then add a handful of kids whose families are from those magical "soccer cultures." Although a tragically high number, particularly children of poorer immigrants, are left behind as well. The result is the tiny base of high-level players from which the US men's national team can draw.

The conclusion is that the US Soccer youth system is most likely still *not* designed for you, for your kid, or for the rest of the kids on your kid's team. They've given up on you before you even started. You're an average American. Average Americans aren't soccer people. Go play baseball.

We've written this book because, of course, we know that culture is not magic. Culture grows from practices, habits, and behaviors, from the games we play and the fun we have. Culture doesn't just shape what we do, but grows out of what we do. Every day. At home. Or, in the case, of soccer, on the fields across the street (if not in the street itself). Culture grows out of our daily practices.

What we do on the soccer field, how kids learn to play, can change the culture. What we've been doing—or not doing—for the last four or five decades, is precisely why the US, despite millions upon millions of kids playing soccer in their youth, has still not become a soccer culture. What is happening at the bottom is, often, not just misguided but utterly backward. So the kids, like Scott, were right to just quit.

When they quit, they take with them little love for the game, because they have little understanding of the game, not to mention even less ability to play it. More importantly, with every kid who quits, the competition among the remaining players is watered down. There are fewer and fewer kids competing with the best players for spots on the best teams. Soon the best kids are abandoned to being "the best" in what is an ever smaller, staler, and status-quo pond.

Consequently, not only do we lose the millions who quit, but we've also ensured that the few thousand who have survived to play in college and even the couple dozen who might get a shot at the pros each year have learned a game developed purely in practice. Why only in practice?

Because when they arrived home every night after practice, there was no one left to play pickup. The rest of their neighborhood chums had stopped playing a few years earlier. When they abandoned the sport, they took very little love for the game with them. The handful of survivors who became elite players and even ended up on the men's national team went home every night to an indifferent culture that did not challenge them. According to the very national team coaches who select them, unsurprisingly, the remaining handful of players are just not good enough.

Picnic, or Weekend at Deep Throat's

But the problems run deeper. What happened to Scott's friends who kept playing soccer on those increasingly exclusive teams every weekend? To see them packing gear into their minivans, Scott might have thought they were heading out for a big family picnic.

In a sense, they were. At least that is what soccer tournaments are supposed to be—a kind of big picnic. An occasion for families to spend time together, take a road trip, eat at restaurants, stay in a hotel, maybe do some shopping. Hmmm, that's starting to sound expensive. What does any of that have to do with soccer?

Good question.

Remember the old Latin saying *cui prodest* ("who benefits")? Or as Deep Throat told Robert Redford and Dustin Hoffman in the Watergate scandal film *All the President's Men*, "Follow the money."

What is a soccer tournament? One extreme would be to call tournaments the worst thing to ever happen to youth soccer. Tournaments mean expensive hotels, meals, tournament T-shirts, slushies, 7:30 am Sunday games, and a car full of fast-food refuse. There is the relatively high risk of overuse injuries from pushing players too hard, potentially playing four games in just two days. How about the pressure and stress to find the next game or that misplaced shin guard left at the hotel? Or the mucked-up championship games played on muddied, torn up fields after a weekend of back-to-back-to-back games, which may be cancelled for rain. What could have been a sensible weekend game is replaced with thirty-six hours of stress. The short time frame instills an inevitable overemphasis on winning that turns parents into absolute loons as their increasingly exhausted child fights for that big plastic cup hanging out there, just four matches away. With the probable forecast of too much sun, cold or rain, tournaments are where ACLs and relationships go to tear apart.

At the other extreme, tournament defenders (read promoters) praise the events as vital for player development. According to this view, tournaments bring the best kids from around the region together, allowing them to compare abilities and to learn from competition. Other sports live by the tournament system: swimming, gymnastics, or various martial arts. Sporting festivals are among the most hallowed occurrences in humanity. Events like the Olympics and even the World Cup have been credited perhaps not with ending wars but at least with postponing them. In this hallowed tradition, youth soccer tournaments are supposed to help kids reach those same inspiring heights of achievement.

Based on our experience with actual US youth tournaments, the arguments in their favor are suspect. Let us temporarily ignore Deep Throat, leave money aside, and begin with player development. Much of our argument in this book is that the more kids play, the better they become. However, the pressure in most youth soccer tournaments breeds an atmosphere that turns the games into nonstop work, not play, or opportunities for technical development.

Some might still argue that pressure can bring out the best in a player. Indeed, this is the very core of the Olympic or World Cup ideal. At those tournaments, once every four years, the youth from across the globe gather in a kind of sacred celebration to inspire feats of bravery and excellence. Hence, the Olympic motto: *higher faster stronger*.

Alas, youth soccer tournaments rarely function like the Olympics. First, instead of a single, sacred, long-term goal, youth tournaments occur in many places and for many teams, almost every weekend. They´re nothing special. Second, in contrast to the Olympics or the World Cup, in most cases these kids have *not* spent a lifetime preparing for this moment. Often, they have not even given it much more than a moment´s thought unless they have to raise funds, which means to deter travel costs, kids (and parents) may have to wash cars or rake some leaves at a group fundraiser.

The games, once and if they start, tend to be tense, tired affairs due to schedules where too many games are crammed back-to-back. After the tournament ends and all the money is spent, only one team goes home happy. Nearly everyone else leaves angry, frustrated, and tired after devoting an entire weekend to losing. This holds true for tournaments at all levels, even the World Cup or the NCAA basketball tournament. However, those events only come once a year or every four years. They confer championship titles with universally acknowledged meaning. For some participants, those titles or the media exposure may be parlayed into real material winnings.

If we return to Deep Throat and follow the money, or lack thereof, 99.9% of kids attending tournaments are never going to become professionals. So where is the money?

The ones earning a living from the tournaments are the tournament directors and sponsoring clubs. They gain hefty entrance fees and may command seed money from municipalities eager to fill hotels and restaurants. Without begrudging enterprising tournament coordinators their source of income, what is the benefit for the kids?

There is still the social and familial argument in favor of tournaments. Families can spend time together, forge friendships with other families, and even establish connections with people and players from other parts of their state or region. Those are certainly desirable aspirations. But which social aspect of the local or regional tournament cannot be replicated by a picnic at the local park? Why are we driving thousands of miles for something available from games and picnics around the corner or in our own back yards?

To make matters worse, these days the tournament model has gone international. Many self-proclaimed premier clubs across the country, and sometimes even larger local clubs, sponsor what we might call "tournament tourism." In the name of club camaraderie and player development, club directors market trips to tournaments in attractive tourist destinations like England, Spain, Italy, or even Brazil or Argentina, where parent and child may worship at soccer shrines like Wembley Stadium, San Siro, or the Maracaná, Through tournament tourism, players and their families can meet and represent their club and nation against players from other countries. They can enjoy a "cultural experience" with sister-city arrangements between towns where dignitaries exchange gifts and take selfies.

Yet, the voice of Deep Throat reminds us to follow the money. The other players and their families must also have the means to participate in these far-flung and expensive affairs. Therefore, the tournaments are less about the game than about having the disposable income to be a tourist. To be fair, there is nothing wrong per se with tourism. Travelling abroad, visiting another culture, struggling with a foreign tongue, navigating an alien culture, and meeting people so different and yet so similar can be life changing. But let's not confuse tourism with soccer development. Let's not pretend that the life skills taught by sport require regional or international travel. Sport is one thing. Tourism is another. And the only reason we ended up outside of Wembley Stadium and $10,000 in the hole was because our kid wanted to kick a ball.

Mediocrity Is Good

So who benefits? Who is behind the system that has given our children such a poor product over the last decades? Or are there larger social and economic forces that the current soccer elite may not be aware of or, more likely, given their educational and professional backgrounds, may not want to understand? When we go overseas, why do we end up wondering, "Why can't we do that in the States? Americans should be able to do anything, right?"

In the film, *Wall Street,* the villain played by Michael Douglas infamously states, "Greed, for lack of a better word, is good." If the film had been about US soccer, the Michael Douglas character might have said, "Mediocrity is good."

Following the money in US soccer leads to the suspicion that the current system and the quality that results from street-style, indigenous-culture football cannot coexist. They are mutually exclusive. Quality soccer, the type of quality prevalent in pick-up games in sports like basketball in gyms around the country, would not require the extra expenses that serve the present system.

As noted in the "No Travel" chapter, the US Soccer system extracts wealth at the lowest levels, where the numbers of participants are the greatest. Instead of making soccer more accessible, the current system has perpetuated a travel, pay-to-play model for adolescents. The introduction of the US Academy Development System in 2007 moved to prohibit elite players from playing in the free, team-sports programs offered by public high schools. Advocates sold this change as a means to increase competition and to afford elite American players access to high-level training. However, in hindsight, the US Development Academy drove an even deeper wedge between a select or self-selected group of elite players and the scholastic setting where American sports culture traditionally thrives.

Most are familiar with the fact that Michael Jordan, arguably the greatest basketball player of all time, did not make his high school varsity squad as a sophomore. This anecdote encourages kids who do not make a team, to keep trying, and more importantly, learn the lessons that sport can teach. Can you imagine the greatest American soccer players of all time, Claudio Reyna or Landon Donovan, not making a high school team anywhere in the country as a sophomore? The US lacks the grassroots quality in the sport for such an occurrence to be remotely possible.

Why has the scholastic route, the Michael Jordan route, been eliminated in US soccer? Unfortunately, under the current cultural and institutional system soccer is defined as somehow elite and foreign. Soccer is not a traditionally popular "American" sport and therefore certainly not the domain of public schools. Instead soccer is the territory of elite clubs and training academies, whose first requirement is a parent with a car (preferably an SUV for carpooling), rather than a kid who can play well. One has to wonder whether the US soccer elite are even aware of their economic path that maximizes profits by limiting access, as if the pricing and supply and demand of youth soccer were the same as beach-front, luxury-hotel rooms.

With just a little more energy, not money, the grassroots could become American soccer's friend. In a free flowing, locally operated system of low intensity, high creativity games; a sports system will naturally reboot itself with each generation, if not with each birth year. Playful, inventive children will be the authors of their own creative destruction, naturally transforming the game as quality skills are learned as part of the culture at local parks and rec programs. Playing soccer could mean no more expense of extramural coaching, new uniforms, fancy shoes, shin guards, golf-green fields, clinics, camps, leagues, or club travel to games and tournaments, to say nothing of trips to exotic soccer meccas like Old Trafford, Camp Nou, or San Siro. If US soccer had quality at the grassroots, then soccer would be just another game, a game that could operate naturally, like basketball, football, or baseball at the local, scholastic level. The destiny of US soccer in international competition would be determined at the high school tryout where America's soccer Michael Jordans would be fighting for a spot on the varsity.

As Americans gain a deeper understanding of the game they will come to understand, as we have, that the current youth system is not producing quality, and that there is little likelihood of an American soccer Michael Jordan or Steph Curry on the horizon. When this happens, soccer participation may decline even further. The suburbanites who have kept US youth soccer afloat all these years will turn elsewhere—lacrosse, ultimate Frisbee, curling?—in search of ways their little ones can truly succeed. With that exodus, so goes the viability of the professional league.

People pay for beauty and quality, and soccer is no exception. American children want to dream of becoming superstars. If it becomes obvious that Americans are so bad at the sport that this can never happen, because the US system cannot produce world-class players, then what will happen? Kids will understand that, if they have dreams of being the best and not just playing in college, then they should play another sport. Arguably an exclusively American one.

Is all lost? To answer this, we turn to the English, who we admit, have taken a bit of a beating in this book. Here, for some redemption, let's bring in their big gun, William Shakespeare. The bard writes, "We are such stuff/ As dreams are made on," often misquoted as "dreams are made of." Merely a preposition, but there is a big difference between the two. We are not made *of* dreams, but rather create our lives *on* dreams. If children cannot create *on* their dreams and realize instead that they live in a country that is by definition a soccer mediocrity, then why play soccer? The sustainability of US soccer depends on the ability to deliver a world-class experience that *children* can make dreams *on*.

If You Build It, Will They Come?

As simple as it might seem to build from the grassroots up, doing so may not be in the perceived short-term economic interests of the system. This is tragic because grassroots quality is certainly in everyone's long-term interests. Creating a culture of players who learn to love the game as kids will allow a commercial US soccer model to focus on what youth players become after they are no longer in the pay-to-play system, namely adults, or in economic terms, paying fans. When we have generation after generation of adults who grew up playing quality soccer, voilà, we will have a soccer culture.

Such a model would not only benefit player development but ironically also solidify the balance sheets of soccer entrepreneurs everywhere. If there were quality in US soccer, then the business model could refocus from the child player as the source of profit to concentrate on developing valuable players and thereby attract spectators. The path to the wallets of adults as spectators is quality that comes with fresh, innovative, exciting, excellent play in a domestic professional league.

The MLS exists and deserves praise for the heroic effort to raise professional soccer from the dead after the 1984 extinction of the old NASL. However, nobody confuses the MLS of 2018 with a world-class soccer league. The decline in youth participation from 2010 to 2016 should be heeded as an emergency call to action by the US soccer establishment. All those kids who are not playing are less likely to become soccer fans. If the MLS lacks an underlying structure of grassroots, quality domestic soccer players, then it lacks long-term sustainability. Currently, MLS rosters are stacked with B-list internationals, former A-list internationals on the verge of retirement, and American players who could not hack it in Europe. Despite recent gains, the MLS business model remains grounded in the Pele-New York Cosmos approach from the 1970s with a short-term goal of year-to-year survival. This model can become sustainable only with the long-term benefits reaped from increasing the quality of US grassroots youth soccer.

High-quality grassroots soccer in the US would offer a surer path to success and sustainability. Our children would no longer have to suffer the travails of the current club, pay-to-play system. Parents would enjoy relief in both the time and expense allotted to what is, after all, just some kids kicking around a ball. The club system could retool. Its cadre of coaches and managers could apply their skills and offer club ball as an extramural, but not defining, step in player development. The money interests could vaunt a viable professional league producing real profits from broadcast rights and merchandising sales worldwide to rival and surpass established American sports.

To be fair, the soccer establishment, the USSF, is retooling. They are offering a grassroots outreach of online courses at basic levels. However, the essentials of the game cannot be truly learned under coaching. Just as the best running backs in American football learned enigmatic subtleties of American football from KTG, the best players in the history of soccer learned playing the street game. The key here is not more stuff or organization, but less. A little handicap training and play in the *shoeless soccer* method described in the "No Drills" chapter will allow the game to teach its barefooted, happenstance-ball, no-grass field self so that Americans can become "fluent" in soccer.

When the Soviet Union put the first man, Yuri Gregarin, into orbit in 1961, the United States responded with the Apollo program and put the first man, Neil Armstrong, on the moon in 1969. In eight years—two World Cup cycles—the United States went from embarrassment to absolute, epochal victory. The moon shot fed an essential narrative in American consciousness based on the competitive urge that harnessed American invention, courage, and will. However, the reaction to World Cup elimination in 2018 was not a moon shot, but fatalism, as if the country were destined never to become a soccer-playing power.

Perhaps the issue is a question of leadership? When leadership does not know what to do, then the question is one of incompetence. As Will Rodgers said about the financial collapse of the 1930s, "It's almost worth the Great Depression to learn how little our big men know."

A quick look at the presidents of the USSF reveals a leadership rooted in the establishment elite, geared toward corporate and institutional benchmarks rather than grassroots quality. The former head of the USSF, Sunil Gulati, holds a doctorate from an Ivy League university, where he also worked as a non-tenureable lecturer. He then occupied an office in the World Bank, an institution well known for goals often more attuned to the interests of governments and corporations than citizens.[1] Gulati's successor, Carlos Cordiero, elected to the USSF presidency in 2018, is yet another Ivy League graduate and a former partner in the Goldman Sachs financial conglomerate, which, like the World Bank, has a reputation for serving the interests of governments and corporations.[2] Since our focus is US youth soccer, we will defer comment on scandals and the corporate culture at FIFA, the governing world soccer federation.[3] Need we say more? Not exactly a group known for championing the interests of the common folk.

The argument in favor of the efforts of Gulati and Cordiero could be like the theme of the 1989 film, *Field of Dreams,* "If you build it, they will come." Before establishment-elite figures like Gulati and Cordiero, US soccer lacked a stable economic structure. The argument is that once a solid economic substructure was established with youth participation, a club system, and a professional league, then the cultural superstructure of quality and a soccer culture would follow. But has this happened?

The Soccer-Industrial Complex

In 1961, President Dwight D. Eisenhower warned of a military-industrial complex whose interests were in the profits from producing weapons rather than in defending the nation. Despite the clear, detailed, and patriotic warning from a five-star general and Allied Supreme Commander in WWII, this complex has only grown in ensuing decades. The United States has not won a complete victory in a war since Eisenhower's speech. Think about it.

We do not want to conflate the problems of youth sports with America's recent defeats in war. However, Eisenhower's warning about a complex pointed out how economic, political, and even spiritual currents can arise to benefit "special interests" more than citizens. American life currently faces "complexes" that are not necessarily from some diabolical plot, but from social and economic realities beyond the capacity of citizens to react. One could debate the action of an education complex with lowered standards and massive student debt. The agriculture-food-industry complex with the dubious quality of hormone, and pesticide-laced food. The pharmaceutical complex with the high cost of medications, opioid addictions, and the black market. The treasury-financial complex, which has seen the value of the US dollar decline a hundredfold against some commodities in the last century. Most disturbing may be the possibility of a medical-consumer complex, where the products sold to consumers may be the cause of diseases like cancer that require specialized health care. If any of these seem far-fetched, no worries. There are obviously plenty to choose from in our highly interconnected, hyper-specialized world. Whatever the case, seen as a whole reveal how easily a variety of apparently independent, disconnected entities unwittingly end up in a financial collusion that ultimately provides little advantage (if not does tremendous harm) to the citizen, patient, consumer—or soccer player—they are each meant to assist.

A measured reaction to the possibility of such obstacles is to try to identify problems and seek solutions, if possible, by asking the ancient Latin question of these systems: *cui prodest* (who benefits)—if in the long term anyone does benefit, that is.

Much of our experience trying to determine the answer to this question in terms of youth soccer comes from our time in the club scene in the American Midwest with a diverse mix of rural, urban, and suburban soccer clubs. No matter the club or the community, our experience has left us with the suspicion, even the realization, that, institutionally and commercially, the American game is ruled by interests protecting livelihoods to the detriment of the development of the game. A cynical motto might be, "If it's broke, don't fix it," if fixing it means I lose my job.

Substructure Determines Superstructure

The substructure of anything determines the superstructure rather than vice versa. The underlying organization and culture of an activity determines its results. Good seeds without soil and water will not produce crops. The argument in this book is that youth soccer cannot rely solely on a viable commercial substructure. The strategy is upside down. What is needed is a a vibrant and

188

broad-scale cultural substructure. The game has to flourish from the bottom up, not from the top down. This does not mean that one must dismantle the nation's entire soccer apparatus, throwing the baby out with the bathwater. However, it does mean stripping away the superfluities that hamstring the game at the most elementary level. US soccer culture needs an environment for the learning of the lessons that are learned in street ball.

Any physical act, including sports, done consciously rather than spontaneously, runs the risk of lacking natural fluidity and grace. Think of the mindless, spontaneous, or unconsciously competent act of brushing one's teeth, combing one's hair, or turning on a light. Consciously planning every step of everyday acts would be absurd. After repetition, these acts become spontaneous, mindless, and are performed in an unconsciously competent manner.[4] The US will not become a soccer-playing nation until American children have an introduction to the game as something which is natural and spontaneous.

In most soccer-playing nations, active kids learn the basics of how to kick a ball at about the same time they learn the basics of washing their hands or eating with cutlery. The game becomes a part of their lives. Toddlers who first waddle on their feet after the sandbox stage are more likely to be able to kick a ball than to catch and throw it back. That is one reason why soccer is universally popular. School recess or the physical education period in many parts of the world consists of a teacher throwing a ball out onto a dirt field or blacktop for the children to play. Being able to play soccer at a pedestrian level occurs naturally through the osmosis of daily existence and peer pressure rather than through instruction.

The street game of the world is a not a skill for the well-born, only attainable through expense. Instead, the game is a part of daily life, the main form of exercise for the majority of children worldwide. An activity ingrained into daily life and imbedded into the myriad of unconscious, automatic acts requires no intricate planning, knowledge, or preparation. When the youth of a nation live in a kick-the-ball culture, they form a coachable pool that may attain higher levels through instruction.

Many American children who may have a more natural cultural introduction to the game never play at higher levels due to the obstacle of the pay-to-play structure of youth club soccer. In club, travel soccer, the deciding factor on making a team is not the ability to play but being able to arrive at practice or game driven by parent who is able to pay. American parents marvel at the natural fluidity with which immigrant kids play the game and wonder why the effort and expense for clubs, coaching, and travel do not produce the same competence. Given the expense in time and money expended on club soccer, parents rightfully expect better results.

No Shoes, No Complex

The US soccer elite have argued that the creativity in the style of poorer countries cannot be institutionally mandated and that something as inherently unstructured as street football cannot be structured. Street soccer is born out of chaos and chance and therefore cannot be quantified and reproduced.[5] But is this true?

Proposals like yearlong seasons and adopting FIFA rules of limited substitutions in high school and college, relegation/promotion for US professional teams, and buyouts for clubs for producing players would require significant work. While we favor all of the above, the grassroots proposals in this book require nothing more than a bit of humility of the part of the people ruling the complex. They could implement them tomorrow and risk only the loss of credibility that might come after acknowledging that they have been selling us a tainted bill of goods for decades.

How complicated would it be to organize inexpensive parks and rec programs for kids just to play on hard surfaces and barefooted under the guidance, not the coaching, of expert youth players they can emulate? Once we create a system that retains the millions who start at age three or five because they love to show up and play, it will be easy to take the next step and develop a soccer culture that is not separated from the high school and college games. Soccer in America could even become a year-round sport with futsal and futebol de salão as indoor games during off-seasons.

The US soccer elite did establish a financial and commercial model for US soccer. However, their model has failed to instill a soccer culture that is sustainable in the long term. For the creation of an American soccer culture, the commercial and economic interests of the US soccer establishment must meld with the interests of citizens and their children, who deserve a quality experience up to world standards.

America has suffered soccer crises before. In 1986, when the US was eliminated by a home 1-0 loss to Costa Rica, the reaction was a flurry of attempts to build the game. The ODP (Olympic Development Program) reached down to the local level of recreational and club level in an attempt to provide extra, quality training to outstanding players in every region. The 1986 attempts to redress US soccer weakness focused on adapting existing structures and methods from established American sports. Parents and children were placed into a structure of parks and rec youth leagues and pay-to-play clubs with a superstructure offering access to high-level coaching. While these reforms had some positive impact, the US is still far from world-class levels.

A successive attempt at reform in 2007 with the US Soccer Development Academy sought to copy European-style, national academy systems, where players identified at the local level could receive higher instruction and competition through travel, bypassing high school and even college soccer. But even this attempt has failed. Each time, solutions are introduced from the top down. Meanwhile, the grassroots, the basic recreational soccer programs where people play, flounder. The result is that the weakness at the bottom has determined the weakness at the top.

Winston Churchill quipped that America always does the right thing, after she has tried everything else. America has tried the commercial approach through the club-travel and pay-to-play system and the restoration of a professional league with the establishment of the MLS. Institutional approaches have been attempted through experiments such as the US Soccer Development Academy. What has not been tried is to focus on the interests of the youngest kids, to focus our best energies at the grassroots level by applying lessons from street and playground ball. Perhaps it is time to recognize the need not for a complex economic approach, but for a simple, playful cultural approach? Under the current system, the sport has revived in the US, but the model relying on travel, fancy uniforms, shoes, grass fields has not created quality at the grassroots. Perhaps it is time to let the elite go their way and do as they will, but let the children play.

So You Say It's Your Birthday or These Go to Eleven

In his book *Outliers*, author Malcolm Gladwell describes how a curiously high percentage of elite hockey players share the same birth months of January and February. Children born near January had an advantage in physical maturity. A difference in physiological development of nine or ten months in a child who is less than a decade old can be very significant, even determinative in youth sports competition. The birth date differential initiated a vicious circle, where children born early in the calendar year benefitted from greater attention, coaching, and opportunities to play than their peers who were a few months younger. Unsurprisingly, the children with a birth month advantage comprised a disproportionate percentage of players scouted for higher-level play.

As part of a reform of US soccer in 2016, the USSF changed age division policies for all youth soccer players. Hailed by some as a sweeping change while decried by others as a travesty, this supposedly significant policy was, in the end, nothing more than a change in the cutoff date for age groups from July 1 to January 1. The reasons were twofold: aligning age groups with the year of a player's birth and aligning US age groups with the rest of the world. That's it.

If every child had been born on January 1st, the rule change would have made some sense. Children with the same birth year are not necessarily at the same stage of physical development. A child born on December 31st would be a year younger than a child born on Jan 1st of the same calendar year. The rule change did not address the problem that Gladwell pointed out in youth hockey. The USSF policy gives children born in January and February an advantage over children born in November or December of the same year. If the rule remains in place, then in about ten years, we may expect to see a number of players on American college or national teams with birthdays in January and February because those players will have enjoyed a physiological advantage over other kids sharing their birth year.

The change from July to January would be comical if not for the children affected. Here, it is difficult to refrain from comment about the decision-making capacity, or lack thereof, of America's establishment elite. What were they thinking? Or more appropriately, were they thinking at all? In the film, *This is Spinal Tap,* a somewhat thick rock guitarist shows off his Marshal stack amplifier explaining that it is louder than other amplifiers because the volume controls go to eleven rather than stopping at ten.

By changing the date from July to January, the USSF was following general FIFA practices as well as other organized sports, which all have a facsimile of the same template for determining age groups. However, the United States is at a disadvantage to soccer-playing nations in cultural terms. To catch up with the world requires innovation. With the age-group division, US soccer could establish a policy that would be an advantage, not just in comparison to other American sports, but with respect to soccer worldwide.

Why can't age group divisions in sport be determined by the player's birthday rather than the birth year? A child who turns ten should move from the nine-year-old team to the ten-year-old team. When she turns eleven, she moves from playing with the ten-year-old team to playing with the eleven-year-olds. No more U9, U10, or U-anything. You play with your age group, which itself, is of course constantly shifting.

In this manner, children will experience being the chronologically youngest as well as the eldest on a team. They would have to adapt from being a new player and possibly the smallest and least experienced at the beginning of their birth year, to being expected to assume a leadership role by the end of their same birth year.

The current age-group divisions are geared toward the interests of coaches and administrators, making their lives easier by having the same group of players year after year. If age groups were determined by birthday rather than birth year, or month within the year, then coaches and managers would have to shift players from one team to another over the course of an annual season. With the uneven distribution of birthdays, certain teams would on occasion have more players than needed while others might have fewer. Players would need to be loaned up at times from lower age groups to fill out rosters. But this is already a very common practice in youth soccer. Gifted children often play up an age group and younger players may be added to rosters as guest players when needed. Another objection may be that such changes on a roster could disrupt team unity and preparation, creating confusion in roles and expectations. But why can't having a child learn to adapt to a new role and expectations be seen as an opportunity for growth and development rather than a hassle for the coach and manager? Whose interests are paramount, the players' or the adults' running the system? One may object that such a proposal is just too complicated to administer with all the carding of players and other official rules that govern today's US youth soccer-industrial complex. But how hard would it be to at least readjust teams every quarter or at most every six months? The current system, as Gladwell has shown, wastes three-quarters of the talent out there.

We would argue that the best interests of children are served by fluid age-group designation by birthday rather than the birth year. Children will be better served by experiencing the full gambit of age and physiology over the course of a playing season, even if that means changing teams. Why should kids suffer perpetual disadvantage due to physiological development determined by a birthday that makes them the youngest player on the team, year after year? Deciding age groups by an arbitrary cutoff date in the calendar year sends the message to children that they are not individuals, but objects, products on the conveyor belt serving the system. Age-group fluidity might even benefit coaches, who would be relieved of pressure to focus on team cohesion and results and could instead concentrate on the technical development of players, which is what they are supposed to be doing anyway.

Promotion for Failure

Despite commercial pressure, the US professional league, the MLS, thankfully, has not removed all of the natural aspects of the game. Proposals to allow timeouts and television commercials have never been accepted. However, the structure of the MLS league does copy the draft model for player acquisition from American professional sports based upon refurbishing failing teams by allowing them first pick (a uniquely American model that is ironically the opposite of the free-enterprise system most Americans claim to celebrate). The beneficiaries of the lose-to-win system—tanking in NBA parlance—are not the local clubs or the grassroots of a national sports culture, but the moneyed interests invested in franchise rights from governing sports associations. In most of the world, the consequences for poor performance by a team are relegation to a lower league, reduced revenues, and the inability to refurbish rosters. When teams around the world fail, they are replaced in upper divisions by teams that have risen against the odds.

Instead, the MLS copies American professional sports model of fiat player designation and franchise approval. These artificial safety nets lessen the severity and natural consequences of defeat. This model was comprehensible when the US market was an expansion experiment in a non soccer-playing country. Soccer became the number-one youth participation sport in the land in the early part of this century thanks to the beauty and simplicity of the game, not because of the requirements of the American commercial model.

We understand that economic realities in the organization of the professional game prevent US soccer from magically transforming overnight. But to paraphrase Lao Tzu: thoughts may become words and words may become actions and actions become character and destiny. How about letting US soccer chart its destiny from some healthy competition? Isn't that the American thing to do?

While it cannot be done overnight, establishing a hierarchy of US soccer leagues from MLS down to the humblest adult recreation league with relegation and promotion should be a clearly stated goal of US Soccer. Relegation and promotion at every level could promote community involvement and pride in their soccer heroes, whether they play at Yankee Stadium or at the local sandlot. If a recreation team wins promotion season after season, why shouldn't that team end up in the MLS?

In leagues around the world, this rarely occurs because richer teams in upper divisions scour lower divisions for talent and reward clubs that produce talent with contract buyouts and transfer fees. This economic incentive rewards local clubs that develop good players, producing a virtuous circle. Player contract buyouts are the greatest incentive from the local to the highest level for player development. If a local team or club develops future professional players, then they should reap the financial rewards.

The Great Seasonal Divide

An unfortunate scheme in US soccer has been to limit high school and college to a single season rather than allowing the sport to run a nine-month season (typically fall to spring with a short winter break), as in the rest of the world. As it currently stands, during the lengthy college off-season, coaches may have only limited contact with players on matters related to technical training but are permitted more contact for physical training. Such restrictions may be logical in American football, where only a few players on a team actually touch the ball during the course of a game. However, in soccer such limitations on honing technical ability are irrational.

The explanation for limiting the soccer season is to allow students, particularly in high school, to participate in other sports. In most soccer-playing nations, soccer is not "a" sport, but "the" sport played year-round. The conflict could be resolved by introducing indoor soccer, futsal (played with a number 4 size futsal ball on a full basketball court) and *futebol de salão* (played with a number 2 size futsal ball on an even smaller court) as separate high school and college sports in winter and in the fall or spring off-season. With these two additional versions of soccer, the year-round-soccer players who aspire to world-class status or who simply love the game can keep honing their craft, while the multisport athletes can get their soccer fix while still playing the other sports they equally love.

Introducing two indoor soccer seasons of futsal and *futebol de salão* as winter and either fall or spring sports would allow children without the means to afford the US club pay-to-play travel system to enjoy the game year-round. Taking advantage of America's high school and college sporting system, a structure absent in much of the rest of the world, could provide a further path for US player development. This would also eliminate the need to concoct specific outreach programs for urban areas or recent immigrants, who could play in an extant scholastic setting. The scouting path would be the same as already employed in basketball and baseball: the tryouts for the junior varsity and varsity high school squads.

What about potential conflicts over space and the question of who gets the gym: basketball, volleyball, or futsal? Please recall the earlier "No Space" chapter, where limiting the space available for play has didactic benefits in soccer. If the school gym is unavailable, then there is always the blacktop, the parking lot, or the dirt lot near the playground.

The MLS should also strive to mimic the fall to spring schedule standard around the world. In its inaugural seasons, the MLS was wary of competing against American football during the fall or against basketball during the winter. The rational was that it was better to compete against one sport, baseball, in the summer, than against two sports in fall and winter. Nevertheless the MLS has slowly been encroaching into the fall-winter territory of American football. The 1995 MLS Cup was held in October. The 2017 MLS Cup was held in December. The MLS is already edging toward a nine-month, weekly game schedule.

Since this is already happening at the professional level, why not apply it to high school and college? Club teams could still engage in a nine-month schedule, which was part of the rationale to form the US Development Academy. Adding opportunities in the public school system would eliminate the fees and travel expenses that many may find onerous, and could provide another source of excellence for US soccer.

16. No Worries

A Tale of Two Teds, or You Say You Want a Revolution?

When we first signed our children up for parks and rec soccer so many years ago, we were stunned at the inferiority of what we saw compared to our experience abroad. We asked ourselves, how can a country historically at the vanguard of achievement, innovation, and invention be so backward in the world's game?

The local teams, we soon discovered, were among the worst in the area, consistently pummeled in lopsided affairs. Not only was our soccer club deficient by world standards, we were subpar even compared to our local peer clubs.

Like good and somewhat naïve citizens, rather than complaining, we figured we'd step up to help fix the problem. Our first reaction was to explain the situation to the local soccer hierarchy, to describe what we had seen overseas, and to propose simple solutions for getting up to speed. They summarily dismissed us.

Even when we attempted to help them win a ten thousand dollar grant to improve the club, they conveniently failed to sign the final form. In their eyes, nothing was broken. This was soccer in our corner of the US and we had better get used to it. And, by the way, they informed us, they knew what they were doing.

The leader of this local old-boys network was Ted, the town's high school coach. Ted also had a monopoly on the local equivalent to parks and rec soccer. He had also made himself the Director of Coaching of the local pay-to-play club. The combination of positions afforded him both a steady income and unilateral decision-making power at every level. He would soon add a lucrative biannual tournament to his own personal soccer-industrial complex. The tournament, like so many already existing in the area, would draw teams from across the region and bring in tens of thousands of dollars.

Good for him. But that didn´t address the quality—or lack thereof—of the soccer our kids were playing.

Not knowing what to do, but unwilling to stand aside while another generation of kids languished in soccer mediocrity, we, naïvely, staged a palace coup. With some phone calls to what turned out to be dozens of disgruntled families, we organized town hall meetings in the best democratic tradition and soon found ourselves the new directors of the old club. We quixotically thought we could still keep the whole thing together with Ted still in the fold. Instead, Ted took his immediate circle of friends and formed his own rival club.

We were nevertheless undaunted and pushed forward with what we thought would be a local soccer revolution. We cast a wide net looking for the best fallow soccer talent in the area. We hired an experienced player and kinesiologist at the local university as our new Director of Coaching. We reached out to the local college´s D-I coaches and players for expertise to raise our players´ game. We even brought in a coach from the Netherlands for a season.

All those efforts, we are pleased to report, raised the general level of play. Within a few years, the club was no longer the laughing stock of the local soccer club scene. A couple of years after that, we began to attract players from outside communities. The best local players opted to stay and play with their friends rather than travel to train and play for one of the "super clubs" in the region. The club even attracted an MLS academy team for players of high school age, creating what seemed to be a symbiosis between community, club, university, and even professional soccer. For a number of years the revolution seemed to be bearing fruit. We´d done it!

Or so we thought. Did we mention we were naïve?

How so?

Before we answer, an aside on the word "revolution": "To revolve" means to return to the initial point of departure. This is not just a linguistic conceit. Political scientists will assure you that most political revolutions do not result in transformations of a system, but rather in their refurbishment under a different guise. The French Revolution replaced the decadent monarchy of Louis XVI with the warmongering dictatorship of Napoleon, after the intervening nastiness of Robespierre and company. Similar patterns have played themselves out over the course of world history in countries from Russia to Mexico. For all the violence, in nearly every case, the rebelling people end up just about where they began. So who were we in our little soccer microcosm to think we could escape the lessons of history?

Today, twelve years after our own soccer palace coup, just as the term "revolution" teaches, despite so much earnest effort and a tremendous amount of work, not much has actually changed. The kids continue to play better soccer than before, but not at levels any better than the general mediocrity typical of US youth soccer.

More depressingly, after initial innovations, successive seasons have seen a reversion to practices that recall the methods and organization of the original high school coach whose uninspiring operation had ignited the first revolt. Indeed, the club´s latest Director of Coaching is none other than the *new* high school coach. And his name? Ted.

We no longer rage. Thankfully, the new Ted is a much more accomplished and professional version of his predecessor. But experience also helps *us* accept the return to the norm. Indeed, experience taught us that many of the original Ted´s decisions and conduct had been rational reactions to the reality of organizing youth soccer in the United States. At the time, we did not have the wisdom— the fruit of experience—to understand that a local revolution in a more broadly broken system would eventually return us to the point of departure.

Worse still, over the course of the decade that we were carrying out our local "revolution," we witnessed the same pattern play itself out time and again from town to town and from club to club across our region. In nearly every case, well-meaning, hard-working parents, local coaches, or community leaders staged coups, formed new splinter clubs, or united old enemies in the perpetual shuffling of deck chairs on the US Youth Soccer Titanic.

Alas, in every case nothing but the uniforms changed. (And expensive uniforms at that.)

The lesson should be clear by now: real improvements will not come by more deck-chair shuffling. Real change must come from the engine room below as the manifestation of a deeper cultural reality. We do not need to take over organizations. We do not need more palace coups.

After all, the palace isn't really the problem. The problem is on the streets—or rather, on the carefully tended grass—below. That is where we can concentrate our energies and channel our naiveté into goodwill. We need to change the way our kids are playing. Then, it will not matter which Ted runs our club. In a few years, he'll have so many good players in his high school program and so much fan interest and the additional resources they bring, that he won't have time to meddle in the local youth teams. What American soccer needs is not organizational revolutions, but a transformation in the way our kids play. It needs a whole new way of doing things.

Going Shoeless: a Modest Proposal

So, as we near the end, the question remains: what to do?

Before responding, it's always good to think money. Money (and wealth) should be an asset, something employed to help children learn, improve, and mature. The costs of the present system, as seen over the course of this book, border on the absurd and are cutting out sections of the population. Wasting money causes stress, which in turn causes health problems, and so on. The roots of the word "sane" mean "healthy." Something that is unhealthy is, then, by definition "insane." Who wants to cut people out from opportunities or to spend more time and money than necessary on anything?

As evident in the preceding pages, right now US soccer is empty-handed. The entire structure of US Soccer, with its massive participation of over three million kids playing in parks and rec, and club ball, resulted in no 2018 World Cup and no steady, reliable stream of world-class players who were products of the grassroots. More gravely, US soccer youth participation has recently suffered a decline of nearly one quarter from 2010 to 2016 with high cost as a major factor. To fix US soccer, is it possible to do things not just cheaper, but cheaper and better?

Our answer throughout this book has been a strong yes to both. In fact, going cheaper really is the only way to get better. US youth soccer has been killing itself for decades with more, more, and then, after a bit of reflection, again even more. Expensive footwear, name-brand uniforms, well-manicured lawns, fancy soccer complexes, paid referees, lengthy travel, and professional coaches litter the youth-soccer landscape. Unfortunately, not only are these expenses almost always unnecessary, but they actually hinder player development. More devastatingly still, the system they uphold undermines the very culture necessary to grow outstanding players. When it comes to youth soccer in America, more and more has become less and less. The time has come at last to take back soccer in this country. To tear off all the expensive trappings, and take the beautiful game back to its naked essence.

Let us conclude with the most barebones of proposals. This is admittedly a not-fully fleshed-out vision of how we could implement simple, inexpensive, and much more beautiful soccer with resources already available in just about every community across America. This vision puts into practice what is already done unofficially in many immigrant communities throughout the land. Take the following as mere food for thought about how to implement the pared-down street soccer the rest of the world enjoys, right here in our own backyards, playgrounds, and, if necessary, even our soccer complexes.

The goal is to simplify how soccer is learned and played at the grassroots and to develop a quality soccer culture. Of course, we cannot be naïve about the realities of our twenty-first century world. America is not a 1950s Brazilian *favela* or 1960s Argentine *villa miseria*. Kids these days don't just play spontaneously in the streets the way Pele or Maradona once did. Just saying kids should play barefooted in a vacant lot free of club and equipment will not make that magically happen. Transforming American soccer will still require a certain amount of physical infrastructure, not to mention a little adult guidance. But how much?

First, let's just be clear one last time about what is *not* necessary.

To become good your child does *not* need:
- Expensive shoes
- An expensive ball
- An expensive coach
- A paid referee
- A fancy uniform
- Regular travel to other cities, and surely not states, for "better" competition
- Weekend tournaments beyond an occasional local event organized by your city for the local kids
- Association with an expensive "select" club

- Well-manicured grass fields or even fancy, artificial-turf fields

So what *do* our children need? This one is much simpler. Here's the list:

- A place to play
- Something to kick
- A better player to play with
- Basic organizational infrastructure

Just four things. Let's take a brief look at each of these.

A Place to Play

To achieve a quality grassroots groundswell that produces a soccer culture in America, we don't need fancy grass fields as much as places to play. All sorts of places. In fact, just about non-grass surface on which a ball will roll. Any park field will do. Even better, any after-school playground blacktop will suffice. Parking lots will do. Patios will work.

Think about what that means financially. After-school blacktops do not need to be built. America is covered with them.

When the blacktop and adjoining grass field become our day-to-day practice and playing surfaces, soccer becomes more local, more community-based, easier to organize, and much more affordable. All the money saved can go to renting or building those (not fancy) spaces that might be necessary for kids playing winter soccer in colder climes.

Something to Kick

Tennis balls? Sure. Nerf soccer balls? Why not? Futsal balls from size one to size four? Of course. And regulation soccer balls, again of all sizes? Most definitely. For good measure, throw in an occasional wrap of old rags. The more variety, the better. That's simple, and almost free.

A Better Player to Play With

Of all these four, this probably needs to be our number-one priority. The joyful, beautiful game is something inspired and then imitated, not coached and then obeyed. Coaching is most effective when the streetwise skills are already in place. Nothing should be more important than locating a handful of the most talented older soccer players in the area and then paying them a bit to share the talents they've honed. The key is talent and a passion for the game, an ability to play with joy, flair, and a touch of genius and trickery. These facilitators must treat the kids the way they would treat a teammate, not a disciple.

Obviously not every community is crawling with retired Neymars and Mbappes. But even local high school kids will do so much more to raise the joy and skill level of our kids than the drills, games, and mini-scrimmages our current cadre of coaches are throwing their way.

Remember, their job isn't to coach. Their job isn't to run drills. Their job isn't to manage or discipline, which may the purview of adult, "director of coaching" or qualified volunteer on the sidelines. The hired player should just play with the kids and give them something to imitate and someone to emulate. Hire a player per practice field (preferably not grass). Then let the children play.

Basic Organizational Infrastructure

Given the current state of US Soccer, this one is the most complex.

- Ages three to eighteen: local parks and rec departments or clubs could provide the general infrastructure for registration, "field" scheduling, and liability issues. Adult supervisors (generally volunteers) would be assigned to "practices" to keep order. A director of coaching at a minimal salary could be hired to maintain quality soccer control over the whole operation and to coordinate the fields where the older role models play with the younger ones. Soccer at this level could consist of three-month seasons (fall, winter, spring) with play indoor (futsal, *futebol de salão*), to allow kids to come and go to other sports but to replicate the regular nine-month season of soccer nations around the world.

- Ages twelve to thirteen: middle schools and junior high schools sponsor soccer teams the same way they currently sponsor football, basketball, baseball, track, and other sports. This should be the first time soccer becomes an 11v11 sport. As an 11v11 sport, soccer must also begin to follow strict FIFA rules regarding substitutions. This 11v11, full-field soccer lasts one three-month season at this age. In the off-season, the middle schoolers would go back to the local parks and rec/club system of blacktop, indoor, futsal, *futebol de salão*, and more casual park soccer, played on smaller fields and with the older facilitators, keeping things touch- and technique-heavy while emotionally light and experimental.

- Ages fourteen to eighteen: high schools continue to offer the single outdoor soccer season (fall or spring). The outdoor season should begin to emulate the full-field, professional game. Games are 11v11 with FIFA substitution rules. High schools could arrange a second and even a third season of futsal or *futebol de salão* seasons in the winter or fall/spring outdoor off-season. Kids could also return to the local parks and rec programs for continued play in a variety of field spaces and surfaces, playing alongside college or adult-age facilitators.

- Ages eighteen to twenty-two: college could become a true breeding ground for MLS and possibly world-class talent by adopting the nine-month FIFA calendar of clubs around the world as well as FIFA substitution rules. To add excitement, American universities could become the first sports system in the US to adopt promotion/relegation. There would only need to be three tiers. The top elite group, a kind of college Champions League—perhaps a top twenty-five of college teams—could travel nationwide for matches against the very best college players in the country. Second- and third-tier university teams would do battle with regional and local rivals, as happens around the world in the lower professional divisions. In each region, the very best would be promoted, while the weakest would suffer relegation. In a couple of years, the most humble NCAA Division-III program could find itself playing in the College Champions League, as often happens with small local teams the world over. If there are limits on substitutions, NCAA Division-III schools would no longer be at a disadvantage to Division-I schools. Think just for a moment of the excitement such an innovation would inject into the college game and what it could mean for smaller communities.

As the nine-month option is likely impractical under NCAA dictates, another proposal would be that four-year colleges, like high schools, could introduce a second and third season of indoor futsal and *futebol de salão*. Soccer could thus become a year-round collegiate sport with the fall for outdoor, full-field soccer, winter for futsal, and spring for *futebol de salão*.

Let the Children (and the Adults) Play

We won´t pretend to know the ins and outs of adjusting the college or high school game and rules or the regulatory challenges in introducing extra seasons for futsal and *futebol de salão*. However, we do know enough about the local level to insist that the measures we're suggesting would be relatively simple to implement. Parks and rec programs, local soccer clubs, and middle and high school sports programs already exist. Parking lots, parks, and open spaces are everywhere. Thus these proposals take advantage of existing infrastructure as well as American traditions. They can be done.

But before we sign off, a final word about pay-to-play. The current system is terribly expensive and has not produced. Still, we shouldn't confuse the people for the system. There are many dedicated people with tremendous talent and experience working within that system. Such talent can and should have a role to play in a renaissance of US Soccer. If they wish to continue along their high-price-tag path, then that is their prerogative. We would prefer that they take the long view and understand that they can benefit from the system we're proposing. They can be the people that team up with the local parks and rec departments. The replication of street ball could be a bonus for club teams, which could focus on organizing extramural games and play in local club leagues. In the long term, the advantage to the clubs is that they would be directing programs with hundreds more kids and significantly less overhead, not to mention the end of the win-at-all-costs pressure that we know from experience drives them all crazy. In many ways, they want out of the current system as much as the rest of us. They know that it's not working. They should see what we're proposing as an opportunity.

Even if no one wants to embrace every proposal laid out in this book, we would argue that the implementation of even just a handful of the changes could make a tremendous difference to your own players, your own team, or even your entire club. We must recognize that if the current system hasn't worked for the grassroots, then the highest levels of US soccer are also at a disadvantage.

Our country already has the infrastructure in place to create a less expensive, less intrusive, and certainly more kid-friendly soccer culture as already practiced unofficially in many immigrant communities. We can create conditions where more kids keep playing longer and with greater creativity. When this happens, and not simply when we produce a few more elite players, the US will become a soccer nation. We will not be competitive in terms of player development and have successful national teams for both men and women without a true grassroots soccer culture.

Finally, what are we really after here with all of this soccer talk? Is it all about watching the US men's national team win a World Cup? That would be fun to watch but would not really improve our lives.

The dream is something bigger. It is that "We Are the World"/"I'd like to Teach the World to Sing" universality that we have experienced playing pickup soccer with people who walked onto the field separated by nationality, age, gender, or class, but became the amalgamation of what they created together. The result was laughs and fun with the occasional scuffle, usually resolved when the contending players put aside their differences because the rest of us were annoyed by the interruption to the game. Such contenders often develop mutual respect and even become friends, the same way it happens with kids.

The approach proposed here may seem like something just for kids, but once a soccer culture develops, why can't there be an unofficial, after-work, adult pickup game on the other side of the blacktop? When kids become good enough, they can join the adult game. The adults will take pride in not cutting any slack, and the kids will benefit from the challenge to raise their game. These kids, in turn, will pass the ability and the lesson on to their children, who will do the same. Then the game will no longer be hindered by the worries and expense of the system. The experience will not even be about soccer, but about friendships and connections between generations. It will be about life.

Acknowledgements

We would like to acknowledge Beth Bentley's help with editing and Michael Richardson's help with cover art and design.

Endnotes

Preface
[1]

https://www.socceramerica.com/publications/article/76121/
new-study-finds-big-drop-in-soccer-participation-i.html.

Chapter 1

[1]"Old habits die hard! Chelsea boss Mourinho clashes with Guardiola over GRASS LENGTH." *Express*. Sept 9, 2014. https://www.express.co.uk/sport/football/508763/Chelsea-boss-Jose-Mourinho-clashes-with-Pep-Guardiola-over-GRASS-LENGTH.

[2] "Brazil's Grass Will Be Like Europe's." *Sefutbol. Official Media Spanish Football Team*. May 23, 2013. http://www.sefutbol.com/en/brazils-grass-will-be-europes.

[3] David Goldblatt. *The Ball is Round: A Global History of Soccer*. (New York: Riverhead Books, 2008), 257.

[4] Please check out histories of soccer like David Goldbaltt's comprehensive *The Ball is Round*, or Jonathan Wilson. *Inverting the Pyramid* (Nation Books, 2013).

Chapter 2

[1]Chevalier G, Sinatra ST, Oschman JL, Delany RM. "Earthing (grounding) the human body reduces blood viscosity-a major factor in cardiovascular disease, "*Journal of Alternative Complimentary Medicine*. 2013 Feb;19(2):102-10. doi: 10.1089/acm.2011.0820. Epub 2012 Jul.

Chapter 3
[1] http://usclubsoccer.org/playersfirst/offerings/la-liga/
[2] Arturo E. Hernandez. *The Bilingual Brain* (Oxford University Press; 2013).

[3] In no way is this section intended to disparage the advantages gained from the study Latin and ancient Greek, which provide the roots for up to 70% of words in technical fields.

[4] Thomas Fleck, R. W. Quinn, D. Carr, W. Buren, V. Stringfield. *The 2015 Official US Youth Soccer Coaching Manual.* http://assets.ngin.com/attachments/document/0069/4246/U SYS_-_Coaching_Manual.pdf.

[5] Bertrand Russell. *A History of Western Philosophy* (New York: Simon and Schuster, 1945).

[6] Edward Gibbon. *The Decline and Fall of the Roman Empire* (Phoenix, 2005).

[7] https://www.theatlantic.com/magazine/archive/2016/03/can -this-man-save-us-soccer/426858/.

[8] W. Timothy Gallwey. *The Inner Game of Tennis: The Classic Guide to the Mental Side of Peak Performance* (New York: Random House Trade Paperbacks, 1997).

Chapter 4

[1] Heather Pedersen, J.A. Pedersen. *What is Montessori? A Basic Guide to the Principles, Practices, and Benefits of a Montessori Education.* (Sandpiper Press LLC, 2008).

Chapter 7

[1] The idea of children being economically worthless but emotionally priceless was first explored by Princeton sociologist Viviana Zelizer, *Pricing the Priceless Child: The Changing Social Value of Children* (Princeton UP 1994).

[2] See Malcolm Gladwell's *Outliers*, for his popularization of the finding that 10,000 hours are required on average to master most skills—artistic, musical, athletic, etc.—at an

expert level.

Chapter 8
[1] William Irwin Thompson, *The American Replacement of Nature: Everyday Acts and Outrageous Evolution of Economic Life* (New York: Doubleday, 1991).
[2] Ibid.

Chapter 9
[1] W. Timothy Gallwey. *The Inner Game of Tennis: The Classic Guide to the Mental Side of Peak Performance* (New York: Random House Trade Paperbacks; 1997).
[2] Joseph A. Schumpeter. *Capitalism, Socialism, and Democracy* (New York: Harper Perennial Modern Classics, 2008).
[3] Roger Boyes. *Meltdown Iceland: Lessons on the World Financial Crisis from a Small Bankrupt Island* (New York: Bloomsbury, 2009).

Chapter 10
[1] Raphael Honigstein. *Das Reboot: How German Soccer Reinvented Itself and Conquered the World* (Nation Books; 2015).

Chapter 13
[1] Geoffrey Douglas. *The Game of Their Lives: The Untold Story of the World Cup's Biggest Upset* (It Books: 2005).

Chapter 14
[1] David Goldblatt. *The Ball is Round: A Global History of Soccer* (Riverhead Books, 2008); Franklin Foer. *How Soccer Explains the World: An Unlikely Theory of Globalization* (New York: Harper Perennial, 2010).
[2] Ivan Waddington and Martin Roderick, "American

Exceptionalism: Soccer and American Football"*The Sports Historian* 16 (1996): 49; A. Markovits, 'The Other American Exceptionalism: Why is there no Soccer in the United States?", *Praxis International* 2 (1988), 125-150.
[3]Dumas Malone.*Jefferson and His Time* (New York: Little, Brown, 1990).

Chapter 15
[1]Bruce Rich. *Mortgaging the Earth: The World Bank, Environmental Impoverishment, and the Crisis of Development* (Beacon Press; 1994).
[2] William D. Cohan. *Money and Power: How Goldman Sachs Came to Rule the World?* (Anchor, 2012).
[3]David Conn. *The Fall of the House of FIFA: The Multimillion-Dollar Corruption at the Heart of Global Soccer* (Nation Books; 2017).
[4] W. Timothy Gallwey. *The Inner Game of Tennis: The Classic Guide to the Mental Side of Peak Performance* (New York: Random House Trade Paperbacks, 1997); Jon Kabat-Zinn PhD. *Mindfulness for Beginners: Reclaiming the Present Moment and Your Life* (Louisville, CO: Sounds True, 2016).
[5]

https://www.theguardian.com/football/blog/2016/jun/01/us-soccer-diversity-problem-world-football.